CAMBRIDGE LIBRARY COLLECTION

Books of enduring scholarly value

Printing and Publishing History

The interface between authors and their readers is a fascinating subject in its own right, revealing a great deal about social attitudes, technological progress, aesthetic values, fashionable interests, political positions, economic constraints, and individual personalities. This part of the Cambridge Library Collection reissues classic studies in the area of printing and publishing history that shed light on developments in typography and book design, printing and binding, the rise and fall of publishing houses and periodicals, and the roles of authors and illustrators. It documents the ebb and flow of the book trade supplying a wide range of customers with products from almanacs to novels, bibles to erotica, and poetry to statistics.

How to Catalogue a Library

Henry Benjamin Wheatley (1838-1917) was a prolific writer on bibliography, literature and the arts. As founder of the Index Society, and editor of *The Bibliographer*, he was also involved in the foundation of the Library Association. In that context he wrote several works on library topics. *How to Catalogue a Library* (1889) was aimed at smaller library collections, as existing systems, such as the manuals of the British Museum library or the Library of Congress, were too elaborate for smaller collections. Wheatley begins by defining the differences between catalogues, indexes and bibliographies, and then compares the existing rules. He discusses the physical form of catalogues and lists the minimum requirements for the catalogue of a small library. He also discusses cataloguing manuscripts and cross-referencing, and provides a useful index of Latin place names. The book contains much on the theory of organisation of information still of relevance today.

T0381753

Cambridge University Press has long been a pioneer in the reissuing of out-of-print titles from its own backlist, producing digital reprints of books that are still sought after by scholars and students but could not be reprinted economically using traditional technology. The Cambridge Library Collection extends this activity to a wider range of books which are still of importance to researchers and professionals, either for the source material they contain, or as landmarks in the history of their academic discipline.

Drawing from the world-renowned collections in the Cambridge University Library, and guided by the advice of experts in each subject area, Cambridge University Press is using state-of-the-art scanning machines in its own Printing House to capture the content of each book selected for inclusion. The files are processed to give a consistently clear, crisp image, and the books finished to the high quality standard for which the Press is recognised around the world. The latest print-on-demand technology ensures that the books will remain available indefinitely, and that orders for single or multiple copies can quickly be supplied.

The Cambridge Library Collection will bring back to life books of enduring scholarly value (including out-of-copyright works originally issued by other publishers) across a wide range of disciplines in the humanities and social sciences and in science and technology.

How to Catalogue a Library

Henry Benjamin Wheatley

CAMBRIDGE
UNIVERSITY PRESS

CAMBRIDGE UNIVERSITY PRESS

Cambridge, New York, Melbourne, Madrid, Cape Town, Singapore,
São Paolo, Delhi, Dubai, Tokyo, Mexico City

Published in the United States of America by Cambridge University Press, New York

www.cambridge.org
Information on this title: www.cambridge.org/9781108021487

This edition first published 1889
This digitally printed version 2010

ISBN 978-1-108-02148-7 Paperback

The Book-Lover's Library.

Edited by

Henry B. Wheatley, F.S.A.

HOW TO

CATALOGUE A LIBRARY

BY

HENRY B. WHEATLEY, F.S.A.

*Author of " How to Form a Library," " The Dedication of Books,"
etc., etc.*

LONDON

ELLIOT STOCK, 62 PATERNOSTER ROW

1889

PREFACE.

THOSE who are interested in library work are constantly asked where a statement of the first principles of cataloguing may be found, and the question is one which it is not easy to answer. Most of the rules which have been printed are intended for large public libraries, and are necessarily laid down on a scale which unfits them for use in the making of a small catalogue. I have divided out the subject on a plan which I hope will commend itself to my readers, and, after discussing the most notable codes, I have concluded

*with a selection of such rules as I
trust will be found useful by those
who are employed in making catalogues of ordinary libraries.*

*Here I must express the hope that
my readers will excuse the frequent
use of the personal pronoun. If the
use of "I" could have been avoided,
I would gladly have avoided it; but
as the main point of the book is the
discussion of principles and theories,
it seemed to me that such value as
the book may possess would be entirely
destroyed if I did not give my own
opinions, founded upon a somewhat
long experience.*

*In dealing with a subject such as
this, I cannot hope to convince all
my readers, but I trust that those
who disagree with my arguments*

will be willing to allow them some force.

The compilation has been attended with constant feelings of regret in my own mind, for almost every page has brought up before me the memory of two men with whom I have at different times discussed most of the points here raised,—two men alike in their unselfish devotion to the cause of Bibliography. Mr. Henry Bradshaw's work was more widely known, but Mr. Benjamin R. Wheatley's labours were scarcely less valued in the smaller circle where they were known, and both brought to bear upon a most difficult subject the whole force of their thoroughly practical minds. I have learned much from both, and I have felt a constant wish to consult them during the preparation of these pages.

All those who prepared the British Museum rules are gone from us ; but happily cataloguers can still boast of Mr. Cutter of Boston, one of the foremost of our craft. Mr. Cutter has prepared a most remarkable code of rules, and has not only laid down the law, but has also fearlessly given the reasons for his faith, and these reasons form a body of sound opinion. May he long live to do honour to Bibliography, a cause which knows no nationality.

H. B. W.

October, 1889.

CONTENTS.

b

Contents. xi

xii   *Contents.*

HOW TO

CATALOGUE A LIBRARY.

CHAPTER I.

INTRODUCTION.

EFORE we can answer the question implied in the title of
this little book, it will be
necessary for author and reader to agree
as to what a catalogue really is.

The word " catalogue " is used to mean
a list or enumeration of men or things.
Thus we have a catalogue of students,
but in actual use we differentiate the
two words, and a list (" a mere list ") is
understood to mean a common inventory,
often in no particular order (although we
can have alphabetical or classified lists) ;

1

while a catalogue implies something fuller and something disposed in a certain order. What the limit of that something fuller and what that certain order as applied to a catalogue of books really are, it will be for us now to consider.

It was formerly very much the fashion for those who knew little of the subject to speak as if nothing was easier than to make a catalogue. All you had to do was to have a sheet of paper and the book to be catalogued before you, and then to transfer the title to the paper. No previous knowledge was necessary. But those who were better acquainted with the difficulties that beset even the cataloguer, realized that Sheridan's joke about "easy writing being damned hard reading" was applicable to the work produced under these circumstances. Since the discussion on the British Museum Catalogue, and the consequent attention to the first principles of bibliography, these ignorant views are not so generally held, but still many· erroneous opinions are abroad. One of these is that the clerical portion of the work of cataloguing or indexing is derogatory to a superior person, and therefore that he should have an inferior person to help him. The superior person dictates, and the inferior person copies down ; and the result in practice is that endless blunders are produced, which might have been saved if one person had done the work.

Another vulgar error is that cataloguers form a guild, with secrets which they wish to keep from the public. This is a grievous mistake. The main object of the good cataloguer should be to make the consultation of his work easy. He knows the difficulties, and knows that rules must be made to overcome these difficulties ; but he does not care to multiply these rules more than is absolutely necessary. The good cataloguer will try to put himself into the place of the intelligent consulter—that is, the person who brings ordinary intelligence to bear upon the catalogue, but has not, necessarily, any technical knowledge. Some persons seem to think that everything is to be brought down to the comprehension of the fool ; but if by doing this we make it more difficult for the intelligent person, the action is surely not politic. The consulter of a catalogue might at least take the trouble to understand the plan upon which it is compiled before using it.

Formerly it was too much the practice to make catalogue entries very short, and to leave out important particulars mentioned on the title-page; but now the opposite extreme of writing out the whole title, however long, is more common. It should be remembered that in the judicious compression of a title-page the art of the cataloguer is brought into play, for any one can copy out the whole of a long title. I cannot help thinking that this latter extreme is caused by some misunderstanding of the relative conditions necessary for the production of bibliographies and catalogues. Of course catalogues form a section of the class Bibliography; but we understand also by the word "bibliography" a collection of titles of books on a special subject, or belonging to a particular literature.

The uses of a bibliography, either of a national literature or of a subject such as

History, are to find out what books have
been written, either by a particular author
or on a particular subject ; to find whether
a certain point is dealt with in a certain
book ; or, it may be, to see whether a
book you possess is the right edition, or
whether it is wanting in some particular.
For these purposes it is most important
to have full titles, and collations with
necessary additional information given in
the form of notes. Very often the particulars included in the bibliography will
be sufficient in themselves to save the
consulter from the necessity of searching
for the book.

The uses of a catalogue are something
quite different. This is in the same
house as the books it describes, and is
merely a help to the finding of those
books. It would be absurd to copy out
long titles in a catalogue and be at the
cost of printing them when the title itself
in the book can be in our hands in a
couple of minutes. Sufficient information
only is required to help us to find the
right book and the right edition. How
far this should be given will be discussed

in a later chapter. It is necessary for us, however, to remember that when the catalogue is printed and away from the library it becomes to some extent a bibliography, and therefore when a library contains rare or unique books it is usual, for love of the cause, to describe these fully, as if the catalogue was a bibliography. This is the more necessary because we are so deficient in good bibliographies. The ideal state, from which we are still far off, would be a complete and full bibliography of all literature, and then cataloguers could be less full in their descriptions, and reference might be made to the bibliography for further particulars. It is a standing disgrace to the country that we have no complete bibliography of English authors, much less of English literature generally.

It has long been the dream of the bibliographer that a universal catalogue might be obtained by the amalgamation of the catalogues of several collections. Thus it was the intention of Gerard Langbaine, Provost of Queen's College, Oxford, and Keeper of the University

Archives, to have made a classified catalogue of the Bodleian Library, and to
incorporate with it all the books not
in the Bodleian but in other Oxford
libraries, public and private, so as to show
at a glance all the books that existed in
Oxford. He died, however, on February
10th, 1657-58, without having carried his
design into execution. Dr. Garnett, in his
valuable paper on "The Printing of the
British Museum Catalogue" (*Transactions*,
Fourth and Fifth Meetings of the Library
Association of the United Kingdom, 1884,
pp. 120-28), gave words to his aspiration
"that the completion of the Museum
Catalogue in print may coincide with the
completion of the present century," and
he continued that no better memorial of
the nineteenth century could be produced
than a "register of almost all the really
valuable literature of all former centuries."
This is very true; but I think that catalogues can only form the groundwork for
bibliographies, and are not sufficiently
satisfactory to supersede them. Moreover,
each country should produce its own
national bibliography.

Mr. Cutter divides libraries into (1) those for study, and (2) those for reading; and this division must always be kept in view. We shall chiefly consider the first division, although it will not be right altogether to pass over the latter. Libraries for reading have been rightly considered in the light of educational institutions; and the various points connected with the information to be given to readers, as to what they should read, and how they should read, perhaps belong more properly to Education than to Bibliography.

As to the order in which the catalogue should be disposed we have considerable choice, and Mr. Cutter has given in the *United States Special Report* (pp. 561-67) a most elaborate classification of the different species of catalogues, but the main divisions are the classified and the alphabetical. Years ago the classified was considered the ideal; but when this ideal was brought down to practice it usually failed, and the result was almost useless. The late Professor De Morgan made the following pertinent remarks on this point :—

" A classed catalogue is supposed to be useful to those who want to know what has been written on a particular subject. Now, in the first place, who are the persons who look at a book list with any such view ? Not beginners in a wide field of research. Did any one in his senses ever go to a library to learn geometry, for instance, and take the subject in a classed catalogue, and fall to work upon some author because he was therein set down ? This attempt to feed the mind *à la carte* would certainly end in an indigestion, if, which is rather to be hoped, it did not begin in a surfeit."[1]

Again :—

" Any one who is willing to trust the maker of a catalogue, however highly qualified, with the power of settling what books he can want in reference to a given subject, is either a person who consults only the most celebrated works, and has nothing to do with research, or one who is willing to take completeness

[1] *Dublin Review*, October 1846, p. 7.

upon trust, and to content himself with blaming another person if he do not reach it." [1]

It is a common mistake to speak of a classified catalogue as a Catalogue Raisonné. A Catalogue Raisonné is a catalogue with bibliographical details and notes, in which the merits or demerits of the books are discussed. Therefore a Catalogue Raisonné can be alphabetical as well as classified. An alphabetical catalogue can be either one of authors, or of subjects, or what the Americans have styled the Dictionary Catalogue. A catalogue of authors will contain the description of anonymous books under headings in the same alphabet, and it may either have an index of subjects, or subject cross-references included in the general alphabet. But as the rules to be considered later on relate chiefly to the catalogue of authors, it is not necessary to say more on this point here. Again, De Morgan has made some excellent remarks on the catalogue of authors :—

"An alphabetical catalogue has this

[1] *Dublin Review*, October 1846, p. 12.

great advantage, that all the works of the same author come together. Those who have had to hunt up old subjects know very well that of all lots which it is useful to find in one place, the works of one given author are those which occur most frequently. Again, those who go to a library to read upon a given subject generally know what authors they want; and an alphabetical catalogue settles the question whether the library does or does not contain the required work of the author wanted. We believe that of those who go into a place where books are collected, whether to read, buy, borrow, (or even steal), nineteen out of twenty know what author they want; and to them an alphabetical catalogue is all-sufficient."[1]

Mr. Cutter has written the history of the Dictionary Catalogue in the *United States Special Report* (pp. 533-39), and he traces it back in America to about the year 1815.

Mr. Crestadoro, in his pamphlet, *The Art of Making Catalogues of Libraries*, 1856,

[1] *Dublin Review*, October 1846, p. 6.

recommended an inventorial catalogue of unabridged titles arranged in no order, but numbered, and an alphabetical index to the numbers of this inventory. The index thus formed was somewhat similar to the Dictionary Catalogue (*United States Special Report*, p. 535). Mr. Bradshaw held very strongly the view that an alphabetical catalogue was an index, and that a full shelf catalogue was the real catalogue ; and few things he enjoyed more than to read through a list of the books as they stood on the shelves.[1] In a letter to me, dated September 9th, 1879, he wrote :—

" It is a cardinal point with me that an alphabetical catalogue of a library is really an index, or should be so, to any other kind of catalogue you choose to make ; while if you once lose sight of this fact you are quite sure to cumber the catalogue up with bibliographical details which are entirely out of place."

[1] I remember very vividly a pleasant day spent in the Pepysian Library with Mr. Bradshaw, under the kindly guardianship of Professor Newton. Mr. Bradshaw was specially delighted with Pepys's own MS. catalogues.

Scientific cataloguing is of modern invention, and to the British Museum it is that we owe the origination of a code of rules—rules which form the groundwork of all modern cataloguing. Good catalogues were made before rules were enunciated, but this is accounted for by the fact that bibliographers, like poets, are more often born than made.

Carefulness must be one of the chief characteristics of the cataloguer, for he will frequently find himself beset with difficulties. Mr. W. F. Poole, the author of that most useful work the *Index to Periodical Literature*, states this very forcibly when he writes :—

"The inexperienced librarian will find the cataloguing of his books the most difficult part of his undertaking, even after he has made a diligent theoretical study of the subject. He will find after he has made considerable progress that much of his work is useless, and scarcely any of it correct." [1]

[1] "On the Organization and Management of Public Libraries" (*United States Special Report,* p. 490).

The cataloguer must not jump to conclusions upon insufficient authority, or, as some persons have proposed, take a short list from the books and amplify the titles from bibliographies. Such a course will lead to endless blunders, and create confusion like that described by Professor De Morgan :—

" Lalande, in his *Bibliographie Astronomique*, wrote from his own knowledge the title of the second edition of the work of Regiomontanus on Triangles, Basle, folio, 1561. He knew that the first edition was published about thirty years before, and so he set it down with the same title-page as the second, including the announcement of the table of Sines, Basle, 1536. Now, as it happened, it was published at Nuremberg in 1533, and there was no table of Sines in it. The consequence is that Apian and Copernicus are deprived of their respective credits, as being very early (the former the earliest) publishers of Sines to a decimal radius. No one can know how far an incorrect description of a book may produce historical falsehood ; but there are few writers who have the courage to say exactly how much they know, and how much they presume." [1]

Before concluding this Introduction it may be well to say something about a few catalogues that have been issued in the different styles. One of the best classified catalogues ever published in England is that of the London Institution, which was first printed in 1835, and completed in 1852.[2] This has indexes of subjects, and of authors and books. The catalogue is very useful as a bibliography ; and as the library was well selected, the reading of its pages is very instructive ; but what shows the general uselessness of a classified catalogue for the work of a library is that in actual practice an alphabetical finding index has been in more constant use than the fuller catalogue.

Of an alphabetical catalogue of subjects an example may be found in that of the

---

[1] *Dublin Review,* October 1846, p. 20.
[2] *Catalogue of the Library of the London Institution, Systematically Classified.* London : 1835-52. 4 vols., royal 8vo.

Library of the Board of Trade, which was published in 1866. Here the authors are relegated to an index, and all the titles are arranged under the main subject. This may be convenient under some circumstances, but it is not satisfactory for general use. The idea of the scheme was due to the late Mr. W. M. Bucknall, then librarian to the Board of Trade; but the catalogue itself was made by the author of this book. The system adopted was to use the subject-word of the title as a heading; but an exception was made in the case of foreign words which were translated. For instance, there is a heading of WOOL. Under this first come all the English works; then the French works under sub-headings of *Laine, Laines,* and *Lainière;* then German under *Schafwoll-handel* and *Wollmarkt.* From these foreign words in the alphabet there are references to WOOL. There is, however, no more classification than is absolutely necessary; and it may be said that if all the books had been anonymous the scheme would have been an admirable one.

The Dictionary Catalogue mostly flourishes in America; but a very satisfactory specimen of the class was prepared by Mr. D. O'Donovan, Parliamentary Librarian, Queensland. It is entitled, *Analytical and Classified Catalogue of the Library of the Parliament of Queensland* (Brisbane: 1883. 4to). The books are entered under author and subject with full cross-references, and all the entries are arranged in one alphabet. There are abstracts of the contents of certain of the books, and references to articles in reviews. In the preface Mr. O'Donovan writes :—

"I have made a catalogue of authors, and index of titles, and an index of subjects, a partial index of forms, and having thrown the whole together into an alphabetical series, the work may be referred to as an ordinary dictionary."

Of the usefulness of the Dictionary Catalogue there cannot be two opinions, but the chief objection is that it is a waste of labour to do for many libraries what if done once in the form of a bibliography would serve for all.

A most important example of this class of catalogue is the *Index-Catalogue of the Library of the Surgeon-General's Office, United States Army,* of which nine large volumes have been issued. This owes its existence to Dr. J. S. Billings, and the publication was commenced in 1880. An enthusiastic friend is inclined to describe it as the best of published catalogues.

Authors' catalogues are the most common, and it would be invidious to point out any one in particular for special commendation.

It is rather curious that the United States, which is now to the fore in all questions of bibliography, should have produced in former times many singularly bad catalogues. There is one classified catalogue which may be mentioned as a typical specimen of bad work. There is an index of authors, with such vague references that in some cases you have to turn over as many as seventy pages to find the book to which you are referred.[1]

[1] *Catalogue of the Library of Congress in the Capitol of the United States of America :* Washington, 1840. 8vo. The third entry in the

The oddities of catalogue-making would form a prolific subject, and we cannot enter into it at the end of this chapter; but space may be found for two odd catalogues which owe their origin to the Secretary of the old Record Commission.

The sale catalogue of portions of Mr. Charles Purton Cooper's library[1] is a literary curiosity. It contains two hundred and fourteen pages, but only one hundred and eighteen of these are devoted to the catalogue of books for sale, and the remaining pages are filled with appendixes which contain many amusing notes. The first appendix consists of a "Catalogue of Books mostly in English, Scottish,

Index is *Abdy*, and the reference "xxix. 215. i.;" xxix. applies to the class, which is *Geography;* the title is to be found in section v., *America;* so that actually seventy pages of the catalogue have to be glanced through before the work of Abdy can be found.

[1] "*Bibliotheca Cooperiana.* Catalogue of Portions of the Extensive and Valuable Library of Charles Purton Cooper, Esq., Q.C. . . . These portions will, by Mr. Cooper's direction, be sold by auction by Messrs. S. Leigh Sotheby and John Wilkinson . . . on Monday, April 19th [1852], and seven following days."

Irish, and Welsh History and Biography
now at Autun, which will be included
in the sale of further portions of Mr.
Purton Cooper's Library unless previously
disposed of by private agreement." On
page 159 is this note to a catalogue
of a collection of grammars and dictionaries "now at Louvain": "My passion
for languages (a very unwise one) ceased
many years ago." Mr. Cooper notes
on page 167, in relation to some books
of miscellaneous antiquities "now at
Brussels," that "the most expensive of the
following works are presents from Foreign
Sovereigns, Universities, Cities, and
Towns, principally in the period 1831—
1840." To the catalogue of miscellaneous
books on page 182 is appended this queer
autobiographical note : "These books,
formerly kept in the house in New Boswell
Court, so long used by me as chambers
(1816—1850), and from whence all my
correspondence as Secretary of Records
was dated (1831—1838), are now in chests
waiting some place of deposit. What will
be their destination I know not. Grove
End Road is let. Denton Court (near

Canterbury, my new residence) has undergone such changes in the hands of its last literary owner (the late Sir Egerton Brydges) that it will hardly afford convenient space for a schoolboy's collection." Mr. Cooper goes on to say : "Indifferent as I am become to the mere possession of books, still the selection was a task with which (having no check but my own will) I dared not trust myself."

The notes to this list are very comical. This book was given to him by a duke, that by a regius professor, another was bought at Fontainebleau, and still another " of a soldier in an English regiment, badly wounded at the disastrous assault upon Bergen-op-Zoom, and then in hospital at Breda." An edition of Aristophanes was bought at Frankfort for nine shillings, and "Lord Harrowby (then Lord Sandon, fresh from Oxford) observed that so cheap a purchase must be a piece of luck rarely occurring." An Edinburgh edition of Livy cost Mr. Cooper five shillings in 1810, "and," he adds, "not a bad bargain, considering the purchaser had not attained his seventeenth year." One of the notes said to be copied from a French book of prayers (1789), is interesting ; but its substance would be said to be incredible if we did not know of the rampant villainy of the times. "In the summer of 1794 (it was somewhat late in the day) two travellers stopped at a chateau in a south-eastern department of France, one of them having a slight acquaintance with the owner of the chateau, who had the misfortune to belong to the ancient noblesse of the country. Both were invited to partake of the family dinner. A dinner which in those circumstances might be considered sumptuous was served up ; and the conversation, as generally happens on such occasions, became more than usually gay. When, however, the dessert was placed on the table, the conversation was suddenly interrupted by one of the travellers taking from his pocket a paper constituting himself and his companion Commissioners of the Convention, and authorizing them to seize the chateau and its contents, and forthwith to guillotine the 'aristocrat,' its proprietor. The reading of this paper was immediately followed by an intimation that a guillotine with the usual assistants had during dinner arrived in the courtyard of the chateau. The repast was discontinued for a few minutes, whilst the two guests hurried their host to the courtyard of his chateau and saw him guillotined; it was then resumed." This curious catalogue has at the end a folding coloured plate of Mr. Cooper's library at Grove End Road, with this note : "The view of the library is here introduced for the purpose of mentioning that Mr. Cooper wishes to dispose, by private agreement, of eight mahogany book-cases of the kind there represented."

In 1856 a sale catalogue of a further portion of Mr. Cooper's library was issued.[1] It consisted of a hundred and fifty-one pages, only thirty-four of which are occupied by the list of books for sale by auction. The rest of the pages are filled

---

[1] "*Catalogue of a Further Portion of the Library of Charles Purton Cooper, Esq., Q.C.* . . . This further portion, deposited with Messrs. Sotheby and Wilkinson in the summer of 1852, will, by Mr. Cooper's direction, be sold by them by auction in the spring of the ensuing year. December 1856."

with lists of books to be disposed of at some future time in some other manner, but there are not notes of the same amusing character as in the former catalogue.

CHAPTER II.

THE BATTLE OF THE RULES.

O Sir Anthony Panizzi we owe rules for the making of cata- logues : perhaps it would be more proper to say the codification of rules, for sound rules must have been in the mind of the compilers of good cata- logues before his time. When one person makes a catalogue, he usually acts upon principles which are known to himself, although he may not have committed them to writing. When several assistants are employed to make a catalogue, it is positively necessary that the compiler in chief, who will be responsible for the whole work, should give directions to his assist- ants, so that they may all work on the same plan.

The famous code of ninety-one rules which was given to the world in 1841 (*Catalogue of Printed Books in the British*

Museum, vol. i., Letter A) had for its foundation a small number of rules originally devised by Mr. Baber [1] (the predecessor of Mr. Panizzi as Keeper of the Printed Books).

Mr. Panizzi was appointed Assistant Librarian in the British Museum in April 1831, and in 1837 he succeeded Mr. Baber as Keeper. As a new general catalogue was now required, a committee was formed to frame rules for its compilation. This committee consisted of Panizzi, Thomas Watts, J. Winter Jones, Edward Edwards, and John H. Parry (afterwards Serjeant Parry). The plan adopted was for each of these gentlemen separately to prepare rules for the purpose, according to his own views. These were afterwards discussed collectively, and when any difference arose, it was settled by vote. When these rules were complete, they were presented to the trustees by Panizzi on March 18th, 1839, with the following memorandum :—

" Mr. Panizzi has the honour to lay

---

[1] *Report of the Commissioners on the Constitution and Government of the British Museum,* 1850, p. 16.

before the trustees the rules, which, under all circumstances, he proposes as advisable to be followed in the compilation of the Alphabetical Catalogue, accompanied by a number of illustrations. Although he is well aware that such rules must necessarily be affected by the haste with which they have been compiled, he ventures to hope they will be sufficiently intelligible to the trustees, and enable them, even in their present imperfect state, to judge of the principles that Mr. Panizzi should wish to see observed. He is fully aware that many cases may arise unprovided for, and that some of these rules and principles may be liable to objections, which may not perhaps appear in other plans, seemingly preferable; but he trusts that what seems objectionable may, on mature reflection, be found in fact less so. He cannot, at present, do more than entreat the trustees to take into their patient and minute consideration every single part, as well as the whole of the plan proposed, and then decide as they may think fit, bearing in mind that, although these rules may, if strictly followed, occasionally lead to what may appear absurd, the same objection, to a perhaps greater extent, may be urged against any other plan, and far greater evils result from a deviation from a principle than from its inflexible application."

The rules were sanctioned by the trustees July 13th, 1839, and printed in 1841. In the note prefixed to the volume of the catalogue then printed Panizzi wrote :—

"The application of the rules was left by the trustees to the discretion of the editor, subject to the condition that a catalogue of the printed books in the library up to the close of the year 1838 be completed within the year 1844."

Panizzi very properly disapproved of the publication piecemeal of the catalogue before it was completed, and eventually he obtained his own way, with the result that the printing was discontinued, and a manuscript catalogue was gradually built up. In the note just referred to he proceeds :—

"With a view to the fulfilment of this undertaking, it was deemed indispensable that a catalogue should be put to press as soon as any portion of the manuscript could be prepared; consequently the early volumes must present omissions and inaccuracies, which it is hoped will diminish in number as the work proceeds."

According to Mr. Fagan (*Life of Sir A. Panizzi*, vol. i., p. 259), the wasteful publication of the volume containing letter A was due to a blunder in the secretary's department. Apparently the order of the trustees was to have the catalogue ready *for* the press by December 1844, instead of which it was intimated to Panizzi that the catalogue was to be printed by that time.

Both Panizzi [1] and Parry [2] pointed out in their evidence before the Commission (1848-49) how wasteful a process it was to catalogue the library by letters instead of cataloguing every book on a shelf at one time. There cannot be two opinions among experienced bibliographers of the absurdity of making a catalogue in such a piecemeal manner, and yet this is a plan

[1] See Questions 4207, 4212, pp. 254-55.
[2] See Question 7223, p. 469.

of proceeding which the inexperienced in cataloguing are frequently found to recommend. Mr. Parry said : " Not only the printing of letter A first do I look upon to be an entire waste, both of time and money—a waste just as much as if the time were thrown away, and just as if the money had been actually thrown away—but the plan of taking those titles from this large body of titles and sending for the books is a serious waste of time. . . . In my opinion, volume A, the volume that is now printed, must be cancelled, if ever the whole catalogue is printed. The reason of that would be, that an immense mass of titles, in the further cataloguing of the succeeding portions of the alphabet, would arise to be catalogued under the letter A, which nobody would have anticipated until the whole library was catalogued." The Commission coincided with Mr. Panizzi's view, and incorporated their opinion on this point in the report. The consequence was that Panizzi was allowed to proceed on his own plan, with the result that, in the first place, a large number of volumes of manuscript titles supplementary to the old general catalogue were produced, and subsequently an entirely new catalogue, superseding the old one.

The history of the catalogues of the British Museum Library is a curious and interesting one. A catalogue prepared by Dr. Maty, the Rev. S. Harper, and the Rev. S. Ayscough was published in 1787 (2 vols., folio). This was soon superseded; and in 1806 Sir Henry Ellis and the Rev. H. H. Baber (then Keeper and Assistant Keeper respectively of the Printed Books), carrying out the instructions of the trustees, commenced the compilation of a new catalogue, which was published in 1813-19 (7 vols. in 8 parts, 8vo). Ellis was answerable for the letters A to F, with P, Q, and R ; and Baber for the remainder of the alphabet.

Now that we have an excellent catalogue of the library, which we owe to the exertions of Panizzi, we are too apt to forget the services of Ellis and Baber as compilers of the very valuable old catalogue. Panizzi took delight in finding faults in this catalogue, and one of the blunders which he pointed out was the entry of a French translation of one of Jeremy Bentham's works, in which the author's name, having been translated in the title-page of the book into French, was transferred in the same form— "Bentham (Jéréme)"—into the catalogue.[1] Doubtless there are many bibliographical mistakes; but it is an excellent practical catalogue, and does the greatest credit to the compilers. Even now, although the print is almost lost in the mass of manuscript, and the volumes are nearly worn out, the copy in the Reading Room may still be used with advantage when a book cannot be found in the more elaborate new catalogue.

In 1847 the Royal Commission, already alluded to, was appointed to inquire into the constitution and government of the British Museum, and the report of the Commission, with minutes of evidence, was published in 1850. This report appeared in a large folio volume of eight

[1] Fagan's *Life of Sir A. Panizzi*, vol. i., pp. 143-44. Mr. Fagan writes "Jérôme," but it is really Jéréme in the catalogue.

hundred and twenty-three pages, which is still full of interest from a bibliographical point of view.

The Commissioners considered arrangements connected with the management which have since been changed, and therefore are of little interest now ; but the evidence chiefly related to the new rules for the catalogue, and resolved itself into an arraignment of Mr. Panizzi's plans, with Panizzi's reply to the arraignment at the end of the evidence. The report shows how unsatisfactory were the relations between the officers of departments, and how strong was the antagonism to Panizzi's rules and arrangements among literary men.

Many authors whom one would have expected to know something of the art of cataloguing showed the most amazing ignorance, and a love for careless work that makes us extremely glad that their cause was defeated. Some witnesses exhibited a dislike to the rules merely because they were rules. Mr. J. G. Cochrane, then Librarian of the London Library, in answer to the question, " Have

you read the ninety-one rules?" said,
"I read some of them, and it appeared
to me that they were more calculated to
perplex and to mystify than to answer
any useful purpose;" and again, when
asked, "Do you object to rules in any
compilation of catalogues?" he said,
"Yes, very much" (p. 460). Further
on in his evidence he said, "I think that
in bibliography, as well as in geography,
it is always advisable to keep as much to
uniformity of system as possible" (p. 464).
But he did not make it clear how uniformity was to be obtained without
rules.

The greatest grievance which "readers"
seem to have had is one which we can
scarcely realize at the present day. Mr.
Panizzi ruled that whoever wanted a book
should look it out in the catalogue, and
copy the title on a slip with the press-
mark before he could receive it. Mr.
Carlyle refused to look out in the catalogue for a pamphlet which he knew
to be in a particular collection. His
account of the matter is as follows :—

"I had occasion at one time to consult

a good many of the pamphlets respecting the Civil War period of the history of England. I supposed those pamphlets to be standing in their own room, on shelves contiguous to each other. I marked on the paper, 'King's Pamphlets,' such and such a number, giving a description undeniably pointing to the volume; and the servant to whom I gave this paper at first said that he could not serve me with the volume, and that I must find it out in the catalogue and state the press-mark, and all the other formalities. Being a little provoked with that state of things, I declared that I would not seek for the book in that form; that I could get no good out of these Pamphlets, on such terms; that I must give them up rather, and go my ways, and try to make the grievance known in some proper quarter" (p. 280).

Dr. J. E. Gray expressed the opinion that the feeling against this rule respecting the press-mark was very general (p. 491). It is necessary to bear in mind that "the old system was, that you merely wrote the title of the book you wanted without the necessity of looking for it in the catalogue. If you wanted a particular edition of it, then you looked in the catalogue for the particular title or date, and the book was brought to you if it could be found" (7684, p. 491).

Although many of the witnesses showed a lamentable ignorance of the principles of sound bibliography, others proved themselves quite capable of setting right the ignorant.

The Right Hon. J. W. Croker, when asked, "Are you of opinion that the labour and difficulties in the management and cataloguing of a library increase merely in the same proportion with its extent?" made this very true observation, "I think the difficulties would increase, I may say geometrically rather than arithmetically" (8734, p. 570).

Mr. John Bruce considered it a fault in the new catalogue that the titles were too full (pp. 417-18); but Prof. A. De Morgan pointed out very clearly the many dangers of short titles (p. 427). Mr. Croker strongly advocated the use of long titles. He said : "There will of course be a few remarkable instances of great prolixity of title-page, which really are worth preserving as curiosities, if for nothing else. But generally speaking there is nothing that is quite safe and satisfactory to a person who goes to look for a book, but a full title ; I will add, a most important consideration in a library like this, which people come to consult ; it has happened to me twice, I think, within the last ten days to find it unnecessary to send for a book that I intended to' apply for, by finding an ample title-page, which showed me that I should not find there what I wanted" (8709, p. 567).

Dr. Gray in his pamphlet (*Letter to the Earl of Ellesmere*, 1849) makes this extraordinary statement: "The works with authors' names, or with false names, should be arranged alphabetically, according to the names of the authors, taking care that the names used should be those that are on the title-pages ; and, if an author have changed his or her name, that the work published under the different names should be in different places in the alphabet" (p. 5).

Mr. Parry gave much sensible evidence, and this point was submitted to him. The question of the chairman (Earl of Ellesmere) was, "Have you heard it proposed that each book should be catalogued under the form of name appearing on the title, without any regard to uniformity, and without regard to the different forms of name adopted by an author, or arising from the different languages in which works by the same author may be printed?" Mr. Parry's answer was as follows: "I have never heard that suggested, except by Mr. Gray. I have read it in Mr. Gray's pamphlet; and I have heard it from Mr. Gray when he was an assistant. . . . I certainly do not wish to be offensive to Mr. Gray, for I have the pleasure of his acquaintance, but I think the thing perfectly absurd. I might be permitted to say, that the noble lord in the chair has published under two or three names; and that I should prefer to see all his lordship's works under one heading, and not scattered in three different places in the Catalogue under the name of Gower, of Egerton, and of Ellesmere. . . . I remember Mr. Gray used occasionally to come and talk about the Catalogue, but it always seemed to me that he had never given any consideration to the subject. It is by no means an easy thing to make a catalogue ; a person to make it, must have a very large and special knowledge of books and of languages " (7338, p. 470).

The witness whose evidence was the most unfortunate for himself was Mr. Payne Collier. He committed himself by submitting some titles which he had made in illustration of his views. There were twenty-five titles, which had been made in the course of an hour. These were handed to Mr. Winter Jones, who reported upon them very fully, with the following result :—

" These twenty-five titles contain almost every possible error which can be committed in cataloguing books, and are open to almost every possible objection which can be brought against concise titles.

The faults may be classed as follows :—
1st. Incorrect or insufficient description,
calculated to mislead as to the nature
or condition of the work specified.   2nd.
Omission of the names of editors, whereby
we lose a most necessary guide in selecting
among different editions of the same work.
3rd. Omission of the Christian names of
authors, causing great confusion between
the works of different authors who have
the same surname—a confusion increasing
in proportion to the extent of the catalogue.   4th. Omission of the names of
annotators.   5th. Omission of the names
of translators.   6th. Omission of the number of the edition, thus rejecting a most
important and direct evidence of the
value of a work.   7th. Adopting the name
of the editor as a heading, when the
name of the author appears in the title-
page.   8th. Adopting the name of the
translator as a heading, when the name
of the author appears on the title-
page.   9th. Adopting as a heading the
title or name of the author merely as
it appears on the title-page—a practice
which would distribute the works of

the Bishop of London under Blomfield, Chester, and London; and those of Lord Ellesmere under Gower, Egerton, and Ellesmere. 10th. Using English or some other language instead of the language of the title-page. 11th. Cataloguing anonymous works, or works published under initials, under the name of the supposed author. Where this practice is adopted, the books so catalogued can be found only by those who possess the same information as the cataloguer, and uniformity of system is impossible, unless the cataloguer know the author of every work published anonymously or under initials.[1] 12th. Errors in grammar. 13th. Errors in descriptions of the size of the book. We have here faults of thirteen different kinds in twenty-five titles, and the number of these faults amount to more than two in each title. . . . When we see such a result as is shown above, from an experiment made by a gentleman of education, accus-

[1] This is the most extraordinary reason ever given. If it were accepted as valid it would settle the question, for under no circumstances could the authors of all anonymous works be discovered.

tomed to research and acquainted with books generally, upon only twenty-five works, taken from his own library, and of the most easy description, we may form some idea of what a catalogue would be, drawn up, in the same manner, by ten persons, of about six hundred thousand works, embracing every branch of human learning, and presenting difficulties of every possible description. The average number of faults being more than two to a title, the total is something startling—about one million three hundred thousand faults for the six hundred thousand works ; that is, supposing the proportion to continue the same."

Then follows a searching examination of each individual title, with the result that any claims to be considered a correct cataloguer which Mr. Collier may have been supposed to have were entirely annihilated.

The Report of the Commissioners enters very fully into the various points raised by the evidence before them, with the result that it was considered advisable that Mr. Panizzi should be given his own way, and that the new catalogue should be completed in manuscript.

The British Museum Rules are, as already stated, printed in the *Catalogue of Printed Books* (*Letter A*, 1841), and in Henry Stevens's *Catalogue of the American Books in the Library of the British Museum at Christmas*, 1856. They are given in Mr. Thomas Nichols's *Handbook for Readers at the British Museum* (1869), under the various subjects in alphabetical order, with a series of useful illustrations. Some slight modifications of the rules have been made since the printing of the catalogue has been in hand, and a capital *résumé* of the rules, under the title of *Explanation of the System of the Catalogue*, is on sale at the Museum for the small sum of one penny.

The strife which was caused by the publication of the rules was gradually quelled, and the British Museum code was acknowledged in most places as a model.

Professor Charles Coffin Jewett published at Washington in 1853 a very careful work on this subject. His pamphlet is entitled, "*Smithsonian Report on the Construction of Catalogues of Libraries, and their Publication by means of Separate Stereotyped Titles, with Rules and Examples.* By Charles C. Jewett, Librarian of the Smithsonian Institution."

Mr. Jewett makes an observation with which all who have considered the subject with attention must agree. He writes :—

" Liability to error and to confusion is . . . so great and so continual, that it is impossible to labour successfully without a rigid adherence to rules. Although such rules be not formally enunciated, they must exist in the mind of the cataloguer and guide him, or the result of his labours will be mortifying and unprofitable."

With respect to his own rules he writes :—

" The Rules which follow are founded upon those adopted for the compilation of the Catalogue of the British Museum. Some of them are verbatim the same ; others conform more to rules advocated by Mr. Panizzi than to those finally sanctioned by the Trustees of the Museum."

The rules are classified as follows :—

pp. 1-45, Titles ; pp. 45-56, Headings ; pp. 57-59, Cross-references ; pp. 59-62, Arrangement ; pp. 62, 63, Maps, Engravings, Music ; p. 64, Exceptional Cases.

The number of rules is not so large as those of the British Museum, and rule 39 stands thus : " Cases not herein provided for, and exceptional cases requiring a departure from any of the preceding rules, are to be decided on by the Superintendent."

Jewett's rules, with some alterations, were adopted and printed by the Boston Public Library.

The *Rules to be Observed in Forming the Alphabetical Catalogue of Printed Books in the University Library*, Cambridge, were drawn up after the authorities had decided to print the catalogue slips of all additions to the library, and also gradually to build up a new catalogue by printing the titles of the books already in the library as they were re-catalogued. These rules were, to a great extent, founded upon those of the British Museum. In the year 1879, Mr. Bradshaw, Librarian, in conjunction with Messrs. E. Magnusson and H. T. Francis, Assistant Librarians, made some alterations in the rules, and as thus altered they now stand, numbering forty-nine.

The rules of the Library Association of the United Kingdom may be considered as somewhat "academical," because they were not made for any particular library. They have gained, however, in importance in that they were adopted by Mr. Edward B. Nicholson, Bodley's Librarian, for the Catalogue of the Bodleian Library. These rules were originally formed for the purpose of making a foundation for a Catalogue of English Literature, as proposed by the late Mr. Cornelius Walford. This catalogue, however, gradually receded into the background, and the rules were adapted to the purposes of a general library catalogue. The rules have been modified at successive annual meetings of the Association.

Although Mr. Nicholson adopted the Library Association Rules in the first instance, he printed in 1882 a set of *Compendious Cataloguing Rules for the Author-Catalogue of the Bodleian Library,* which has since been added to, and the number of rules is now sixty.

We have, in conclusion, to take note of by far the most important code of rules after that of the British Museum. I allude of course to the remarkable second part of the *Special Report on Public Libraries in the United States* (1876), which consists of " Rules for a Printed Dictionary Catalogue, by Charles A. Cutter." This work stands alone in the literature of our subject. Not only are the rules set out, but the reasons for the rules are given. This is usually considered as a dangerous proceeding, and it requires a man with the clear-headedness and mastery of his subject for which Mr. Cutter is distinguished to carry out such a scheme with success. I am not prepared to agree altogether with the principle of the Dictionary Catalogue, or with all the reasons for the rules—in fact, some of them are highly stimulating, and prove strong incentives to argument; but it would be difficult to find anywhere in so small a space so many sound bibliographical principles elucidated.

It is now nearly fifty years since the British Museum Rules were published, and at the present time we can scarcely understand the antagonistic feeling with which these rules were then received. We can now see how much we are indebted to them. To their influence we largely owe the education of the librarian in the true art of cataloguing, and the improved public opinion on the subject; and to them we owe the noble Catalogue of the British Museum, which is a remarkable monument of great knowledge and great labour combined. We are therefore bound to do honour to the memory of Panizzi, who planned the work and endued with his spirit the many distinguished men who have followed him and completed his work.

CHAPTER III.

PRINT *v.* MANUSCRIPT.

HERE has been much discussion on the relative advantages of Print and Manuscript. Panizzi's objection to print was a sound one, as he considered that no titles should be printed until the catalogue of the whole library was completed. When this time came the objection was no longer valid, and arrangements were made in due course for printing the catalogue by instalments. Before this was decided upon there were some who insisted upon the actual superiority of manuscript over print; but this was really absurd, because, if the extra cost of printing can be defrayed, there must be great advantage in the clearness and legibility of print, as well as in the saving of space caused by its use.

Mr. Parry, with his strong common sense, advocated, in 1849, the use of the

4

printing-press. He said in his evidence :
"I think the Catalogue ought to be printed;
not merely for the purposes of the library,
and of reference out of the library, but
also because I think the Catalogue of this
library is a work that ought to be in every
public institution where men of letters
resort, either here, on the Continent, in
America, or in any other part of the
civilized world ; still, it ought not to be
printed until the whole of the books are
catalogued up to a certain time. I say
'up to a certain time' because the whole
of the books never can be catalogued in a
library where there are constant accessions.
But a limit may be fixed, and when that
limit is reached and the whole of the
books within that limit are catalogued I
would then print the Catalogue, and not
before. I have said before that the volume
of letter A must be cancelled; that is in-
evitable. Nobody after this Catalogue is
completed, no librarian, no man of the
most ordinary literary acquirements, would
presume to print the Catalogue without
cancelling this volume : that arises from
the circumstance that, as the cataloguing

goes on, thousands of works will turn up
as necessary to be inserted in letter A." [1]

Mr. Parry added, that in ordering this
partial printing the trustees gave way to
pressure from without, which he defined
very justly as "a sort of ignorant im-
patience for a catalogue by persons who
do not really understand what a catalogue
is or what a catalogue should be."

Dr. Garnett read a very interesting
paper on "The Printing of the British
Museum Catalogue," before the Library
Association, at the Cambridge meeting, in
1882, in which he tells how the present
system of printing came about.

Mr. Rye, when Keeper of the Printed
Books, strongly urged the adoption of
print; but Dr. Garnett adds, "Other
views, however, prevailed for the time;
and when, in October 1875, the subject
was again brought forward by the Treasury it fell to my lot to treat it from
a new point of view, suggested by my

---

[1] It must be thoroughly understood that this
catalogue of letter A is in itself an excellent piece
of work. Its shortcomings are entirely due to
incompleteness caused by premature printing.

observations in my capacity as superintendent of the reading-room. I saw that, waiving the question as to the advantage or disadvantage of print in the abstract, it would soon be necessary to resort to it for the sake of economy of space. There were by this time two thousand volumes of manuscript catalogue in the reading-room, exclusive of the catalogues of maps and music. There would be three thousand by the time that the incorporation of the general and supplementary catalogues was complete. Hundreds of these volumes in the earlier letters of the alphabet were already swollen with entries, and required to be broken up and divided into three. Sooner or later every volume would have undergone this process. By that time there would be nine thousand volumes of manuscript catalogue, three times as many as the reading-room could contain, or the public conveniently consult. The only remedy was to put a check upon the growth of the catalogue by printing all new entries for the future, and to mature meanwhile a plan for converting the entire catalogue

into a printed one. I prepared a memorandum embodying these ideas, and entered into the subject more fully, when, in
January 1878, it was again brought forward by the Treasury. These views,
however, did not find acceptance at the
time. . . . The question was thus left for
Mr. Bond, who became Principal Librarian
in the following August. As Keeper of
the Manuscripts, Mr. Bond's attention had
never been officially drawn to the catalogue of printed books, but as a man of
letters, he had formed an opinion respecting it; and I am able to state that he
came to the principal librarianship as
determined to bestow the boon of print
upon the Catalogue and the public, as to
effect the other great reforms that have
signalized his administration." [1]

Dr. Garnett, near the end of his paper,
said, "My aspiration is that the com-

[1] *Transactions* of the Fourth and Fifth Annual
Meetings of the Library Association, 1884, pp. 122-
23. In the discussion which followed the reading of this paper, I ventured to speak of the
British Museum having been converted to the
advantages of printing. Mr. Bullen in his speech
said: "There were those in the Museum, Mr.

pletion of the Museum Catalogue in print may coincide with the completion of the present century;" and I believe he still holds the opinion that this is possible and probable.

Mr. Cutter enters very fully into this question of *Printed or Manuscript?* in his elaborate article on "Library Catalogues" in the *United States Report on Public Libraries*, 1876 (pp. 552-56). The advantages of a printed catalogue he states under five heads: "(1) that it is in less danger of partial or total destruction than a manuscript volume or drawers of cards;" "(2) that it can be consulted out of the library;" "(3) that it can be consulted in other libraries;" "(4) that it is easier to read than the best manuscript volume, and very much easier to consult. A card presents to the eye only one title at a time, whereas a printed catalogue generally

Garnett and himself among them, who, long before the present time, advocated printed, in contradistinction to manuscript, catalogues. As a manuscript catalogue was one of the greatest advantages to a library, so a printed catalogue must of course be of a hundred times greater advantage" (p. 207).

has all an author's works on a single page.
Time and patience are lost in turning over
cards, and it is not easy either to find the
particular title that is wanted or to com-
pare different titles and make a selection;"
" (5) that several persons can consult it at
once."

The disadvantages are stated by Mr.
Cutter under three heads : " (1) that it is
costly ; " " (2) that a mistake once made is
made for ever, whereas in a card catalogue
a mistake in name or in classification or
in copying the title can be corrected at
any time ; " " (3) it is out of date before
it is published. As it cannot contain the
newest books, the very ones most sought
for, fresh supplements are continually
needed, each of which causes an additional
loss of time and patience to consulters.
The average man will not look in over
four places for a book ; a few, very per-
severing or driven by a great need, will go
as far as five or six. It becomes necessary
therefore, if the catalogue is to be of any
use, to print consolidated supplements
every five years, and that is expensive."

Of the advantages the main one is No. 4,

and of the disadvantages the only one of any importance is, it seems to me, No. 1.

As to disadvantage No. 2, it is more apparent than real. A mistake in print will of course remain for ever in the copies of the catalogue outside the library, but it can easily be corrected in the library copy either in manuscript or by reprinting the single title in which the mistake occurs. The card catalogue cannot be used outside the library, and the catalogue in the library can be as easily corrected whether it be printed and pasted down on pages or arranged on cards. The two are equal in this respect. Disadvantage 3 is the stock objection. But what does it really come to? He who consults the catalogue of a library away from that library knows that a given book is there if he finds it in the catalogue; but if it is not in the catalogue, he does not give up hope, but either visits the library or sends to know if the book he requires is in. He is no worse off in this case than if there had been no printed catalogue; and in the former case he is much better off. The library copy of the catalogue can be kept

up as well in print as it can be in manuscript, and here at all events there will
only be one alphabet. It will therefore
be a question for the consulter alone
whether it is better worth his while to
consult several supplements than to go
straight to the library. For the purposes
of the library, it is quite unnecessary to
reprint or consolidate your supplements,
because your library copy of the catalogue
will always be kept up to date. If the
library is a lending one, the subscribers
will probably insist upon having new
catalogues, as the supplements become
too numerous; but this is only an additional
instance of the advantages of a printed
catalogue.

A printed catalogue should never be
added to in manuscript, as this causes the
greatest confusion; and, moreover, it is not
necessary. It is quite possible to keep up
a catalogue in print for many years; and
even when worn out, if the printed sheets
have been kept, a working catalogue can
be made up afresh without printing again.
The plan adopted by my brother, the late
Mr. B. R. Wheatley, is so simple, that it

seems scarcely necessary to enlarge upon
its merits ; but as it has not been generally
adopted, I may perhaps explain it here
with advantage. It will be seen by the
specimen on page 59, that each page of
the library copy of the catalogue is divided
in two. On the left-hand side is pasted
down the catalogue as it exists at the
time, and the right-hand side is left for
additions. These additions may be
printed as annual supplements, or they
may be printed from time to time at short
intervals on galley slips on one side only,
without being made into pages. This can
be done as suits the best convenience of
all concerned ; and it is just as easy to have
the titles printed frequently as to have
them copied for insertion in the library
copy of the catalogue. The ruled columns
are for the press-marks, and these are
arranged on the outside of each column
for purposes of symmetry. It is not
advantageous, as a rule, to print the press-
marks in the catalogue, although this is
done in the case of the British Museum.
There are two advantages in having two
columns of type on one page. One is that

Case.	Shelf.			Case.	Shelf.
B	1	LE BRETON (Anna Letitia). Memoir of Mrs. Barbauld, with Letters and Notices of her Family. Sm. 8vo, London, 1847.		N	5
B	2	—— Correspondence of Dr. Channing and Lucy Aikin (1826-1842). Sm. 8vo, London, 1874.	LIDDELL (Henry Geo.), and Robert SCOTT. A Lexicon, abridged from "Liddell and Scott's Greek-English Lexicon"; 14th edition. Sm. square 8vo, Oxford, 1871.		
G	4	MCNICOLL (David H.). Dictionary of Natural History Terms, with their derivations, including the various orders, genera, and species. Sm. 8vo, London, 1863.			

there is a saving of space, and the other is that it is easier to keep the alphabet in perfect register if it becomes necessary to insert a page. However well arranged a library copy of a catalogue may be, it will probably become congested in some places before the whole catalogue requires re-adjustment. Now suppose each page contains only one column of print, and the left-hand page is left for additions. When both pages are full, and it is necessary to insert a leaf for fresh additions, it is clear that the correct order of the alphabet will be thrown out. But if there are two columns on each page, then the additional leaf will introduce no confusion; for the recto of the additional leaf will range with the verso of the old leaf, and the verso of the additional leaf with the recto of the next leaf in the book. The only difference will be that you will have to run your eye along four columns instead of two.[1]

The advantage of this plan is that the

[1] I find that the merits of this plan are not so self-evident as I thought, for my friend, Mr. J. B. Bailey, Librarian of the Royal College of Surgeons, who has had experience of a double columned catalogue, prefers a single column

library catalogue can be actually kept up
for any length of time without any reprinting. When the catalogue is filled up, and
there is no room for any additions, the
whole may be pasted down afresh as in
the first instance, always presuming that
copies of the catalogue and its supplements have been retained.

Sometimes the pasting down of the
print is delegated to the binder; but it
should be done either by the librarian
himself, or at all events under his eye, for
much judgment and knowledge are required for the proper leaving of spaces
where the additions are likely to be the
thickest.

Another advantage of this plan is that
a practically new library catalogue may
be made up from old printed catalogues. Some five-and-twenty years ago,
the Athenæum Club possessed a worn-

with the *verso* of each page left for additions.
I allow that there may be advantages in the
latter, but as an octavo page of print is very
narrow it is wasteful of space to have only one
column. Where it is no disadvantage to have a
catalogue in several volumes, this question of
space need not be considered.

out catalogue of its library. Supplements were printed, and I laid down in one alphabet a catalogue of the whole, which has lasted to the present time, although I believe it is pretty well worn out now. There were certain difficulties to be overcome, for the catalogue and its supplements were not made on the same system.

Card catalogues have been strongly advocated by some, and they present many advantages if used while the catalogue is growing in completeness ; but for use when the catalogue is completed they cannot compete in convenience with the plan just described. It takes much longer to look through a series of cards representing the works of a given author than it does to run the eye down a page of titles.[1]

Professor Otis Robinson, in his article on " College Library Administration " (*United States Report on Public Libraries,*

[1] Mr. Cutter gives some useful information respecting card catalogues and the drawers used for keeping the cards, in his article on "Library Catalogues" (*United States Report on Public Libraries,* pp. 555-60).

p. 512), writes thus on the adoption of card catalogues in the United States :—

" In some of the largest libraries of the country the card system has been exclusively adopted. Several of them have no intention of printing any more catalogues in book form. In others cards are adopted for current accessions, with the expectation of printing supplements from them from time to time. I think the tendency of the smaller libraries is to adopt the former plan, keeping a manuscript card catalogue of books as they are added, without a thought of printing."

This system of cataloguing has not taken hold of the English mind, although it has been adopted at the Bodleian Library by Mr. Nicholson, and at the Guildhall Library. The growth of this fashion appears to me as something almost incomprehensible, and one can only ask why such a primitive mode of arrangement should be preferred to a book catalogue. I can scarcely imagine anything more maddening than a frequent reference to cards in a drawer; and my objection is not theoretical, but formed on a long course of fingering slips or cards. If the arrangement of the catalogue is constantly being altered, it may be convenient to have cards; but when a proper system has been settled at the beginning, this cannot be necessary. When additions only have to be considered, these can be inserted into the book catalogue, so that the catalogue may last for many years. The use of a duplicate set of titles on cards for use in arrangement, which can be arranged and rearranged as often as required, is quite another matter. This plan is adopted at the Bodleian.

Varieties of type help the eye to choose out what it requires, and there is much saving of time in consulting a good printed catalogue instead of a good manuscript one. This is not a matter of opinion merely, but can be proved at once by consulting the printed volumes of the British Museum Catalogue against the volumes still in manuscript.

Before the details of printing are finally settled it is well to pay particular attention to the typographical arrangement, as a catalogue will be all the more useful as it is well set out.

A very ingenious scheme for the stereotyping of catalogue titles was published by Mr. C. C. Jewett, Librarian of the Smithsonian Institution, in 1850.[1]

The mode of carrying out the plan is explained as follows :—

" 1. The Smithsonian Institution to publish rules for the preparation of catalogues.

" 2. To request other institutions intending to publish catalogues of their books to prepare them according to these rules, with a view to their being stereotyped under the direction of the Smithsonian Institution.

" 3. The Smithsonian Institution to pay the whole *extra* expense of stereotyping, or such part thereof as may be agreed on.

" 4. The stereotyped titles to remain

---

[1] "A Plan for Stereotyping Catalogues by Separate Titles, and for forming a General Stereotyped Catalogue of Public Libraries in the United States." *Proceedings of the Fourth Meeting of the American Association for the Advancement of Science, held at New Haven, Conn., August* 1850 (8vo, Washington, 1851).

the property of the Smithsonian Institution.

" 5. Every library uniting in this plan to have the right of using all the titles in the possession of the Smithsonian Institution, as often as desired for the printing of its own catalogue by the Institution; paying only the expense of making up the pages, of the press work, and of distributing the titles to their proper places.

" 6. The Smithsonian Institution to publish as soon as possible, and at stated intervals, general catalogues of all libraries coming into this system."

It is not necessary here to explain how the stereotyped slips were to be manufactured, as the explanation will be found in the original paper.

A scheme of an allied character was propounded by the late Mr. Henry Stevens, who read a very interesting and amusing paper before the Conference of Librarians in 1877 on " Photo-Bibliography; or, A Central Bibliographical Clearing House" (*Transactions*, pp. 70-81). Mr. Stevens wrote :—

" My notion is that every book, big

and little, that is published, like every child, big and little, that is born, should be registered, without inquiry into its merits or character. . . . I ask the attention of this Conference of Librarians to a word on the necessity of cataloguing every book printed ; the importance of printed card catalogues of old, rare, beautiful, and costly books, and how to make them on a co-operative or universal system, which, for lack of a better term, I shall for the present call ' photo-bibliography.' For carrying out this project a Central Bibliographical Bureau or Clearing House for Librarians is suggested."

The author goes on to say :—

" From the days of Hipparchus to the present time, the stars have been catalogued ; and to-day every bird, beast, fish, shell, insect, and living thing, yea every tree, shrub, flower, rock, and gem, as they become known are scientifically, systematically, and intelligently named, described, and catalogued. In all these departments of human knowledge there is a well-ascertained and generally acknowledged system, which is dignified as a science."

But no such system of registering books
has ever been attempted. The cure for
this negligence is then suggested :—

"This isolation and waste of vain
repetition, it is believed, is wholly unnecessary. There is no royal road, it has
been said, to knowledge. He who would
attain the goal must learn to labour and to
wait, for knowledge is locked up mainly
in books, appropriately termed works.
There is, however, a short cut with a pass-
key in universal or co-operative bibliography, a simple system of arrangement
by which may be economized the labours
of hundreds who are cataloguing over and
over the same books."

Mr. Stevens's special contribution to
this great object was the use of reduced
photographs of the title-pages of rare and
curious books. The adoption of this
plan would help on vastly the study of
bibliography.

The strong feeling as to the waste of
time occupied in the constant repetition
going on in cataloguing the same book
in different libraries crops up again and
again, and surely we shall in the end be

able to elaborate some scheme which will meet such a universally felt want. Professor Robinson was one of the earliest to protest against this waste, and his attention was called to it when inspecting various card catalogues. He found similar cards being repeatedly reproduced, and he suggested that by some system of co-operation this waste of labour might be reduced (*United States Report on Public Libraries,* pp. 512-14).

Two practical suggestions have been made. One is that every publisher should place in each copy of each book issued by him a catalogue slip made upon a proper system which has been settled by competent authorities, so that there may be a satisfactory uniformity ; and the other that each government should catalogue every work published in its country. The former plan is scarcely likely to be undertaken systematically by all publishers, but the latter one might be carried out in connection with the ratification of copyright privileges. Every publication should be registered, and a copy submitted at the registration office. A part of the business of this office should be to issue periodically proper catalogue slips of every work registered, on a settled plan that had been well thought out by experts. The authorities of Stationers' Hall ought long ago to have been instructed to issue lists of all the books registered there ; and if they were not prepared to undertake the duties indicated by the new Registration Law, the office might possibly be transferred to the British Museum with advantage. If England initiated such a scheme, other nations would probably follow its lead. At present the Catalogue of the British Museum, as now published, to some extent fulfils the required conditions ; but much that is published in Great Britain even escapes through the meshes of the Museum's widespread net.

However much printed catalogues may be superior to manuscript ones, the latter must always be used in a large number of cases, especially for private libraries ; and therefore it may be well to say a few words here respecting the preparation and keeping up of a manuscript catalogue.

There are two ways of making and keeping up a new catalogue. The one is that adopted at the British Museum, which was suggested simultaneously by the Right Hon. J. Wilson Croker, and by Mr. Roy, one of the Assistant Librarians in the Printed Book Department. The catalogue slips are lightly pasted down into guarded volumes, the ends being left unpasted, so that the slips can easily be detached with the help of a paper-knife if it be needful at any time to change their position.

The other plan is to copy out fairly the titles on one side of sheets of paper, proper spaces being left, as well as the whole of the opposite page for additions. These sheets are afterwards bound into a volume or volumes. The former plan is the best for a large and a constantly increasing catalogue ; but the latter plan is more satisfactory for an ordinary private library, as it forms a more shapable and better-looking volume. From experience it may be said that a catalogue of this

Case.	Shelf.		Size.	Date.
10	B	HAYDN (Joseph). Haydn's Dictionary of Dates and Universal Information, relating to all ages and nations ; 16th edition, containing the History of the World to the autumn of 1878, by Benjamin Vincent. *London.*	*8vo*	1878

kind, in which proper spaces have been
left, will last for many years ; and should
it become congested in any one portion,
it is quite easy to rewrite those pages
on a larger scale, and have the volume
rebound.

A specimen of how paper should be
ruled for a manuscript catalogue made on
the latter plan is given on page 72. The
columns at the right-hand side of the
paper, for size and date, add to the clearness of the catalogue, as well as making
the page look neater. The most useful
size is about 1 ft. 5 in. high by 11½ in.
wide—the size of Whatman's best drawing
paper, which can be used with advantage.

CHAPTER IV.

HOW TO TREAT A TITLE-PAGE.

IN this chapter we shall discuss the various points that arise in connection with the transference of the title of a book to the catalogue slip, and for convenience we shall treat the subject under the following main divisions: 1. Author; 2. Headings other than Author Headings; 3. The Title; 4. Place of Publication; 5. Date; 6. Size Notation; 7. Collation.

Before dealing with these points it is necessary to give the cataloguer a warning not to take his title from the outer wrapper. The title-page only must be used, but in cases where there is no title-page, and it becomes necessary to copy from the wrapper, this must be clearly stated. Wrappers and title-pages of the same book often differ, and a neglect of the above rule has sometimes caused a

confusion in bibliographies by the con-
version of one book into two.

AUTHOR.

With the title-page of the book to be
catalogued before us, our first care is to
find the author's name. If there is no
author's name, we must put the book
aside for consideration later on. First
of all, therefore, it is necessary to answer
the question, What is an author?

Mr. Cutter's definition is as follows:
" Author, in the narrower sense, is the
person who writes a book; in a wider
sense, it may be applied to him who is
the cause of the book's existence, by
putting together the writings of several
authors (usually called *the editor*, more
properly to be called *the collector*). Bodies
of men (societies, cities, legislative bodies,
countries) are to be considered the
authors of their memoirs, transactions,
journals, debates, reports, etc." This is
a fair definition, about which there can
be no dispute, down to the word *collector ;*
but the latter portion requires much

consideration, and we shall have to deal with it further on.

First let us consider some of the questions which arise respecting the person who writes the book. If we suppose his names to be John Smith, we have the matter in its simplest form for a small catalogue, and we write at the head of a slip of paper—SMITH (JOHN).

But in the case of a large library, the very simplicity causes a difficulty. There are so many different John Smiths, that it becomes necessary to find out some means of distinguishing them. At the British Museum explanatory designations, such as *Schoolmaster, Bibliographer*, etc., are added; but this point belongs more properly to arrangement, which will be discussed in the sixth chapter of this book.

All authors' names, however, are not so simple as those of John Smith, and one of the greatest difficulties is connected with compound names.

A few years ago the rule respecting these compound names might have been stated quite simply, thus : " In foreign names take the first as the catch-word, and in English names take the last." But lately a large number of persons have taken a fancy to bring into prominence their second Christian name, when it is obtained from a surname, and, adding a hyphen, insist on being called Clarkson-Smith, Sholto-Brown, or Tredegar-Jones. Now here is a great difficulty which the cataloguer has to face. Take the case of John Clarkson Smith. His family name may be Clarkson, and the Smith added as a necessary consequence of obtaining a certain property, in which case he properly comes under C; but he may just as likely be a Smith, who, having been named Clarkson at his christening, thinks it advantageous to bring that name into prominence, so as to distinguish himself from the other Smiths. Probably, to still further carry on the process, he will name all his children Clarkson, so that in the end it will become practically a compound surname. The cataloguer, therefore, needs to know much personal and family history before he can decide correctly. If we decide in all cases to take the first of the names hyphened together, we shall still meet with difficulties, for many persons, knowing the origin of the Clarkson, will insist on calling our friend Smith.

On this point the British Museum rule is :—

" Foreign compound surnames to be entered under the initial of the first of them. In compound Dutch and English surnames, the last name to be preferred, if no entry of a work by the same person occur in the Catalogue under the first name only."

Cutter rules as follows :—

" 16. Put compound names :

" *a.* If English, under the last part of the name, when the first has not been used alone by the author.

" This rule requires no investigation and secures uniformity ; but, like all rules, it sometimes leads to entries under headings where nobody would look for them. Refer.

" *b.* If foreign, under the first part.

" Both such compound names as GENTIL-BERNARD, and such as GENTIL DE CHAVAGNAC. There are various exceptions, as FÉNELON, not SALIGNAC DE

LAMOTHE FÉNELON; VOLTAIRE, not AROUET DE VOLTAIRE. Moreover, it is not always easy to determine what is a compound surname in French. A convenient rule would be to follow the authority of Hoefer (*Biog Gen.*) and Quérard in such cases, if they always agreed,—unfortunately they often differ. References are necessary whichever way one decides each case."

The Library Association rule is :—

" 32. English compound surnames are to be entered under the last part of the name; foreign ones under the first part, cross-references being given in all instances."

The Cambridge rule is as follows :—

" 4. [English] compound surnames to be entered under the last part of the compound, unless when joined by a hyphen.

" 9. [Foreign] compound names to be under the first part of the compound."

It will be seen that, although all the lawgivers are agreed upon the general principle, they do not entirely settle the difficulty which has been raised above.

Probably it will be best for the cataloguer to settle each individual case on its own merits, and to be generous in the use of cross-references. It is dangerous to be guided by hyphens, because they have become absurdly common, and many persons seem to be ignorant of the true meaning of the hyphen. One sometimes even sees an ordinary Christian name joined to the surname by a hyphen, as John-Smith.

Prefixes present a great difficulty to the cataloguer, and here again a different rule has to be adopted for foreign names to that which governs English names. The broad rule is that in foreign names the article should be retained, and the preposition rejected ; and the reason for this is that the article is permanent, while the preposition is not. A prefix which is translated into the relative term in a foreign language cannot be considered as a fixed portion of the name. Thus Alexander von Humboldt translated his name into Alexander de Humboldt when away from his native country. For the same reason prefixes are retained in English names. They have no meaning in themselves, and cannot be translated. There is a difficulty in the case of certain cosmopolitan Jews who use the " De " before their names. This is so with the Rothschilds, who style themselves De Rothschilds ; but when a British peerage was conferred on the head of the house the " De " went. Under these circumstances we must consider the " De " as a foreign prefix, and reject it.

There is probably no point in cataloguing which presents so many difficulties to the inexperienced as this one connected with prefixes, and yet it is one upon which the lawgivers are far from being so clear as they ought to be.

Mr. Cutter's rule is the fullest, and that of the Library Association the vaguest.

Mr. Cutter writes as follows :—

" 17. Put surnames preceded by prefixes :

"*a.* In French, under the prefix when it is or contains an article, *Les, La, L', Du, Des ;* under the word following when the prefix is a preposition, *De, D'.*

"*b.* In English, under the prefix,

6

as *De Quincey, Van Buren,* with references when necessary.

"*c.* In all other languages, under the name following the prefix, as *Gama,* Vasco de, with references whenever the name has been commonly used in English with the prefix, as *Del Rio, Vandyck, Van Ess.*"

This is all the Library Association have to say :—

"31. English and French surnames beginning with a prefix (except the French *De* and *D'*) are to be recorded under the prefix ; in other languages, under the word following."

The British Museum rule stands thus :—

"12. Foreign names, excepting French, preceded by a preposition and article, or by both, to be entered under the name immediately following. French names preceded by a preposition only, to follow the same rule : those preceded by an article, or by a preposition and an article, to be entered under the initial letter of the article. English surnames, of foreign origin, to be entered under their initial, even if originally belonging to a preposition."

The Cambridge rules are as follows :—

" 8. German and Dutch names, preceded by a preposition or an article, or both, to be catalogued under the name, and not under the preposition or article.

" 9. French, Italian, Spanish, and Portuguese names, preeeded by a preposition only, to be catalogued under the name ; those preceded by an article, or by a preposition and an article forming one word, to be catalogued under the article or combined preposition and article."

The point was fully considered by the Index Society ; and as the rule laid down by the Council is full and clear, I venture to give it here in addition to those above.

" 5. Proper names of foreigners to be alphabetically arranged under the prefixes

Dal.	as	*Dal Sie.*
Del.		*Del Rio.*
Della.		*Della Casa.*
Des.		*Des Cloiseaux.*
Du.		*Du Bois.*
La.		*La Condamine.*
Le.		*Le Sage.*

but not under the prefixes

D'.	as *Abbadie*	not *D'Abbadie.*
Da.	*Silva*	*Da Silva.*
De.	*La Place*	*De La Place.*
Von.	*Humboldt*	*Von Humboldt.*
Van.	*Beneden*	*Van Beneden.*
Van der.	*Hoeven*	*Van der Hoeven.*

It is an acknowleged principle that when
the prefix is a preposition it is to be rejected,
but when an article it is to be retained.
When, however, as in the case of the
French *Du, Des,* the two are joined, it is
necessary to retain the preposition. This
also applies to the case of the Italian
Della, which is often rejected by cataloguers. English names are, however, to
be arranged under the prefixes *De, Dela,
Van,* etc., as *De Quincey, Delabeche, Van
Mildert,* because these prefixes are meaningless in English and form an integral
part of the name."

We must be careful not to invent an
author by misreading a title, as was done
by the cataloguer who entered the *Relatio
felicis agonis* of certain martyrs as the
work of one Felix Ago.[1] This is by no

[1] *Quarterly Review,* vol. lxxii., p. 8.

means an unnecessary caution, for several
imaginary authors have found their way
into biographical dictionaries by the
blundering of title-readers.

The British Museum rule by which
Voltaire is entered under *Arouet* and
Molière under *Poquelin* has been so often
criticised that I scarcely like to refer to
it here; but as these are very striking
examples of an irritating rule, I feel
bound to allude to them. Mr. Jewett,
in forming his rules, felt bound to place
Arouet le jeune and Poquelin under the
only names by which they are known,
viz., Voltaire and Moliere; and to cover
his departure from rules he was following, he made this note: "The family
name of an individual is to be considered
that which he has or adopts for himself
and his descendants rather than that which
he received from his ancestors—his family
name, not his father's." This, to a great
extent, covers the case; for we are bound
to take for our catalogue the name by
which an author decides to be known, and
by which he always is known. It is not for
us to rake up his family history. Panizzi,

however, specially answered the objection
made to his treatment of Voltaire. He
said that Lelong, in his *Bibliotheque
Historique de la France,* while Voltaire
was alive, entered him under Arouet; and
in answer to the question, " Mr. Tomlinson
states that the family name of Voltaire was
Arouet, a name which the writer himself
never used, and by which he was scarcely
known ? " Panizzi added, " The first thing
that occurred in his life was, that he
was sent to prison as Arouet, as the supposed writer of certain satirical verses
against the Regent ; and if you look at
the index to the best edition of St. Simon,
you will not find Voltaire at all. You will
find M. Arouet. We put it under Arouet,
but there is a cross-reference from Voltaire.
I believe Mr. Milnes pointed out the
advantage of this, because, he said, the
greatest harm that can arise is, that if you
look under ' Voltaire ' you find that you
are sent to ' Arouet,' but if we are not
consistent we mislead every one " (p. 675).
This is an answer, but I do not think it
will be accepted as a satisfactory one.
The reference could as easily be made the

other way, and no one would be misled. References should be from the little known to the better known, and not the reverse way. We may pay too high a price for consistency in cataloguing.

By the rule that an author should be placed under the name by which he is best known, Melanchthon will be under that name and not under Schwartzerde, Œcolampadius not under Hausschein, Xylander not under Holzmann, Regiomontanus not under Müller. The tersest reason I know for this rule is that of Professor De Morgan : "As the butchers' bills of these eminent men are lost, and their writings only remain, it is best to designate them by the name which they bear on the latter rather than on the former."

We shall sometimes come upon a title in which the author appears as the Bishop of Carlisle, or the Dean of Chichester; and before making the heading for our catalogue slip we shall have to look in a book of dignities, or almanac, or directory to find out the surname of the bishop or the dean. These titles can no

more be treated as names than could the
Mayor or Recorder of Brighton be registered under the name of that place. This
rule is clear, and one that is universally
adopted ; but in another case, which
is supposed to be similar, the lawgivers
have, I think, gone very wrong. It has
become general to place peers under their
family names instead of under their titles.
This rule is in direct opposition to the
clear principle of placing an author under
the name by which he is best known, and
under which he is most likely to be sought
for. The majority of peers are known
only by their titles, and therefore if they
are placed under their family names they
are placed under the worst possible heading. Readers of history know that the
great· Duke of Marlborough began to
make a figure as Colonel Churchill, but
most persons know him only as Marlborough, and when they wish to find
whether a certain catalogue contains his
Despatches, they do not wish either to be
referred to Churchill or to have to look for
his family name in a peerage. The titles
of noblemen and the names of the sees

of bishops have really little in common. The title is practically the man's name, and he has no other for use; but a bishop never loses his name.

The British Museum rules, and those of the Cambridge University Library, direct that noblemen shall be placed under their family names. At Cambridge there is the further rule that, " in the case of dukes of the blood royal who have no surname, the title is to be taken as the leading word." The necessity for this exception condemns the original rule.

The Library Association and Bodleian rules adopt the common-sense plan of entering noblemen under their titles; and Mr. Cutter gives some excellent reasons for doing this, although he cannot make up his mind to run counter to a supposed well-established rule.

Mr. Cutter writes :—

" STANHOPE, Philip Dormer, *4th Earl of Chesterfield.* . . . This is the British Museum rule and Mr. Jewett's. Mr. Perkins prefers entry under titles for British noblemen also, in which I should agree with him if the opposite practice

were not so well established. The reasons
for entry under the title are that British
noblemen are always spoken of, always
sign by their titles only, and seldom put
the family name upon the title-pages of
their books, so that ninety-nine in a
hundred readers must look under the
title first. The reasons against it are that
the founders of noble families are often
as well known—sometimes even better—
by their family name as by their titles
(as Charles Jenkinson, afterwards Lord
Liverpool; Sir Robert Walpole, afterwards
Earl of Orford); that the same man
bears different titles in different parts of
his life (thus P. Stanhope published his
*History of England from the Peace of
Utrecht* as Lord Mahon, and his *Reign
of Queen Anne* as Earl Stanhope); that
it separates members of the same family
(Lord Chancellor Eldon would be under
Eldon, and his father and all his brothers
and sisters under the family name, Scott),
and brings together members of different
families (thus the earldom of Bath has
been held by members of the families
of Shaunde, Bourchier, Granville, and

Pulteney, and the family name of the present Marquis of Bath is Thynne), which last argument would be more to the point in planning a family history. The same objections apply to the entry of French noblemen under their titles, about which there can be no hesitation. The strongest argument in favour of the Museum rule is that it is well established, and that it is desirable that there should be some uniform rule."

Sovereigns, saints, and friars are to be registered under their Christian names. Upon this point all the authorities are agreed. The British Museum rule is :—

" IV. The works of sovereigns, or of princes of sovereign houses, to be entered under their Christian or first name, in their English form.

" VI. Works of friars, who, by the constitution of their order, drop their surname, to be entered under the Christian name ; the name of the family, if ascertained, to be added in brackets. The same to be done for persons canonized as well as for those known under their first name only, to which, for the sake of distinction, they add that of their native place or profession or rank."

The Cambridge rule 12 is the same as the British Museum rule VI., but worded a little differently.

The Library Association rule appears in a highly condensed form, thus :—

" 28. All persons generally known by a forename are to be so entered, the English form being used in the case of sovereigns, popes, ruling princes, oriental writers, friars, and persons canonized."

As usual, Mr. Cutter is more explicit. His rule is as follows :—

" 13. Put under the Christian or first name :

" *a.* Sovereigns or princes of sovereign houses. Use the English form of the name."

The direction, " Use the English form of the name," was a concession to ignorance. When it was given, that form was almost alone employed in English books. Since then the tone of literature has changed; the desire for local colouring has led to the use of foreign forms, and we have become familiarized with Louis,

Henri, Marguerite, Carlos, Karl, Wilhelm, Gustaf. If the present tendency continues, we shall be able to treat princes' names like any other foreign names; perhaps the next generation of cataloguers will no more tolerate the headings *William*, Emperor of Germany, Lewis XIV., than they will tolerate Virgil, Horace, Pliny. The change, to be sure, would give rise to some difficult questions of nationality, but it would diminish the number of the titles now accumulated under the more common royal names.

"*b*. Persons canonized.

"*Ex.* THOMAS [à Becket], *Saint.*

"*c*. Friars, who, by the constitution of their order, drop their surname. Add the name of the family in parentheses, and refer from it.

"*Ex.* Paolino da S. Bartolomeo [J. P. Wesdin].

"*d*. Persons known under their first name only, whether or not they add that of their native place or profession or rank.

"*Ex.* PAULUS *Diaconus*, THOMAS *Heisterbacensis.*"

Here are, I think, two points which are open to question. Doubtless it is far better to use the correct forms of foreign Christian names than the English forms, and when the initial is the same there can be no objection ; but it is not satisfactory to separate the same name over different letters of the alphabet. It must be remembered that the name in a catalogue is a heading taken out of its proper place on the title-page, for the sake of convenience, and therefore there is no impropriety or show of ignorance if these headings are in English.

As to the practice with respect to the names of saints, I think the rule is a good one ; but there must be some exceptions, and Mr. Cutter's example I should treat as an exception.

Thomas à Becket, Archbishop of Canterbury, is known to most men as Becket, and under that name they would look for him. The mere fact that the Roman Catholic Church chose to canonize him does not seem to be a sufficient reason for putting him under the heading of Thomas (St.), where no one but an ecclesiastic would think of looking for him.

These rules go on to deal with Oriental authors, who are to be placed under their first names. This rule is, perhaps, the safest, if we know nothing of Oriental names; but it will often need to be departed from, and Mr. Cutter's suggestion is therefore a good one. He writes: "Graesse's *Lehrbuch einer allgemeinen Literärgeschichte* is a convenient guide in this matter; he prints that part of the name by which Arabic writers are commonly known in a heavier type than the rest." This is not a subject which is likely to trouble the general cataloguer much, and in the case of a multitude of Oriental works special information must be sought.

Something must now be said about Christian names. These should not be contracted, but written in full, unless a special system of contraction is adopted. Mr. Cutter suggested in the *American Library Journal* that the most common Christian names should be represented by an initial with a colon after it; thus, Hart, G: H:, would read Hart, George Henry; but Hart, G. H., would be read as usual, and G. H. might stand for any names. Mr. Cutter contributed a list of the abbreviations of Christian names which he adopted to the *American Library Journal* (vol. i., p. 405).

There is a great difficulty connected with the arrangement of Christian names in large catalogues, such as that of the British Museum, which must be overcome by means of cross-references. Suppose a certain work which you require is written by one Charles Raphael Smith. You are pretty sure to have the name given as Raphael Smith, and in consequence you will seek for the name in the secondary alphabet R, while it will really be found under C, and to this position you probably have no clue.

Sometimes cataloguers take a great deal of pains to discover a Christian name that an author has persistently dropped, but this in general only gives everyone unnecessary trouble.

In foreign titles it is not always easy to distinguish between Christian and surnames. For instance, there are a large number of surnames in Spanish which are formed from Christian names in the same way as Richards is formed from Richard. Thus Fernando is a Christian name, but Fernandez or Fernandes is a surname. Again, in Hungarian and some other languages, the surname is placed first, and is followed by the Christian name. The surname is, in fact, made into an adjective, as if we spoke of the Smithian John instead of John Smith.

A difficulty arises when authors change their name, for it is necessary to bring all the works by an author under one heading, and the question must be settled whether the first or the last name is to be chosen.

The British Museum rule is :—

"XI. Works of authors who change their name, or add to it a second, after having begun to publish under the first, to be entered under the first name, noticing any alteration which may have subsequently taken place."

This is a very inconvenient rule, as it frequently causes an author to be placed under his least known name. For instance, in the British Museum Catalogue the

7

works of Sir Francis Palgrave are entered under Cohen, a name which not one in ten thousand persons knows to have been the original name of the historian. The reverse plan is therefore more generally adopted. Thus the Cambridge rule is :—

" 7. Persons who change their names, or add a second name or a title, to be catalogued under the final form (being a surname) which their name assumes, the previous entries being gathered under this heading by means of written entries on the slip."

And Cutter writes :—

" 15. Put the works of authors who change their name under the latest form, provided the new name be legally and permanently adopted."

Intimately connected with this change of name by authors is the case of authoresses who are married after they have commenced to write. Here the most convenient plan is to adopt the husband's name, except in those cases where the authoress elects to continue her maiden name. In this, as in many other cases, it is not advisable to go behind the writer's own statement in the title-page. If the author is consistent in using one name on all his or her works, there is no need to seek out a name which he or she does not use. The cataloguer's difficulty arises when different names are used at different periods of life ; and, as his main duty is to bring all the works of an author under one heading, he must decide which of the different names he is to choose as a heading.

Mr. Cutter's rule is :—

"Married women, using the surname of the last husband, or if divorced, the name then assumed. Refer.

"I should be inclined to make an exception in the case of those wives who continue writing, and are known in literature, only under their maiden names (as Miss FREER, or Fanny LEWALD), were we sure of dealing with them only as authors, but they may be subjects; we may have lives of them, for instance, which ought to be entered under their present names."

The Library Association rule is rather ambiguous :—

" 29. Married women and other persons who have changed their names to be put under the name best known, with a cross-reference from the last authorized name."

The case of married women is carried by the British Museum rule respecting change of name which is quoted above, with the inconvenient result that Mrs. Centlivre, the playwright, who is only known by that name, appears in the British Museum Catalogue under the name Carroll.

Having dealt with some of the difficulties of modern names, we will pass on to consider some of the points connected with classical names. There is little difficulty connected with Greek authors, as they usually had but one name; but as a mixture of alphabets cannot be tolerated in the headings of catalogues, we must use the Latin form of these names, as Herodotus, not Ἡρόδοτος. In this case, besides the inconvenience of different alphabets, we should have the author known to us all as Herodotus under the letter E, if we adopted the original form.

There is more to be said with respect to the names of Roman authors. Mr. Cutter's rule is :—

" 18. Put names of Latin authors under that part of the name chosen in Smith's *Dictionary of Greek and Roman Biography*, unless there is some good reason for not doing so."

This rule is very good as far as it goes, but a general rule may be laid down which will save the cataloguer from the need of consulting Smith, except in very difficult cases. Most Latin authors have three names—the prenomen, which answers to our Christian name ; the nomen, or family name ; and the agnomen. In the case of Quintus Horatius Flaccus, Quintus is the prenomen, Horatius the nomen by which the author is and ought to be known, and Flaccus is the agnomen. But in the case of Cicero we have incorrectly taken to call him by his agnomen, although our ancestors correctly called him by his nomen, Tully. The same thing may be said of Cæsar, whose family name was Julius. But we must be content to follow custom in these cases. Besides the agnomen some men had a cognomen, or strictly personal name, and some had two prenomens ; so that it is not safe to take the middle of three names as the nomen for certain. In some cases the prenomens of authors have been lost, and others have come down to us without agnomens.

Having dealt with the chief difficulties connected with the arrangement of the name of an author when there is no doubt about who the author is, we must now pass on to those cases where there is some difficulty in deciding as to the authorship of a book. Many titles are purposely misleading. Thus a letter addressed to some celebrated person is made to appear as if it were written by that person.

A well-known county history in six volumes, quarto, is constantly quoted as the work of one who never wrote it, on account of the misleading character of the title-page. This book is entitled, " *Collections for the History of Hampshire. By* D. Y. With Original Domesday of the County, and an Accurate English

Translation. . . . By Richard Warner. . . ."
The second volume contains the Domesday, and this alone is edited by Warner.
In his *Literary Recollections* (1830), the
Rev. R. Warner remarks on this. He
writes : " A circumstance somewhat sin-
gular arose out of the publication of
*Hampshire, extracted from Domesday
Book,* as the volume formed the foundation of one of the most barefaced piracies
ever committed on the literary property
of an unfortunate author " (vol. ii., p. 267).

Mr. Cutter's remark, already referred to,
that he who is the cause of a book's existence should be treated as the author, is
a perfectly just one. Thus we are in the
habit of using the word " editor " rather
loosely. According to the work done by
the so-called editor, we shall arrange the
book under his name or not. If a man
takes a book which already exists and
edits it with notes, he establishes no
right to have its title placed under his
name. For instance, if the original book
has an author, it goes under his name ;
or if it is anonymous, it is treated by the
rule that governs anonymous books. To

adopt any other system would be to distribute various editions of the same book under different headings. On the other hand, if a man collects together various pieces, and forms an entirely new and substantive work, he should be treated as the author, because without his initiative the book would have no existence. Hakluyt's *Principal Navigations of the English Navigators*, Purchas's *Pilgrimes and Pilgrimages*, and Pinkerton's *Collection of Voyages and Travels*, are special cases about which no one would doubt; but the cataloguer will come upon cases where he may have some difficulty in deciding.

Mr. Cutter enters very fully into the points relating to corporate authors, some of which are of considerable difficulty. First among corporate authors are societies and institutions who publish proceedings ; but these will be treated in the sixth chapter, under the heading of Transactions. There are, however, many other publications of corporate bodies which do not come under this heading, such as Acts, Laws, Resolutions, Reports, etc. It is scarcely worth while to discuss this point very fully here, as this class of book is only to be found in the largest libraries, where the rules are settled. Moreover, they will sometimes require to be treated differently, according to the class of library in which they are included.

According to the rules of the Cambridge University Library, they are arranged under the general (or superior) heading of *Official Publications.*

Academical dissertations frequently offer considerable difficulties to the cataloguer, and as the recognized authorities are not so clear in their rules upon this subject as they might be, I venture here to introduce the substance of a paper which my brother, the late Mr. B. R. Wheatley, read before the Library Association in 1881 :—

ON THE QUESTION OF AUTHORSHIP IN ACADEMICAL DISSERTATIONS.

In the " title-taking " of these dissertations the difficulty is not in their "subjects," which are sometimes confined even to a single word, but it is in the choice of their authors' names : whether the præses, the respondent, the proponent or defendant is to be chosen. It may perhaps be thought that I am fighting with a shadow, but when it is considered that the seventh of the *Rules for Cataloguing* printed by the British Museum, copied afterwards into Cutter's Rules, and since, I find, adopted by the Library Association, is that "The Respondent or Defendant of a Thesis is the Author, except when it unequivocally appears to be the work of the Præses," and that nevertheless in some special catalogues, such as Pritzel's *The saurus*, Haller's *Bibliothecæ*, etc., and in the catalogues of the Linnæan and some other Societies' libraries, the rule has been generally adopted that the præses is the author, or at least that he takes that position from the dissertations being en tered under his name—and that in a large number of collections of these dissertations, this latter rule has been frequently favoured —it will be allowed that this shadow puts on a substantial appearance, and has sufficient reality in it to bear a practical discussion. In placing before you some examples from title-pages, in illustration of the question, I must apologize for taking them entirely from works connected with Medicine and its allied sciences, as being the class more immediately ready to my hand for reference.

Before entering on the bibliographical part of our subject, you will allow me to quote, from Watts' *On the Improvement of the Mind*, a short summary of the method of scholastic disputation: " The tutor appoints a question in some of the sciences to be debated amongst his students ; one of them undertakes to affirm or to deny the question and to defend his assertion or negation, and to answer all objections against it; he is called the *respondent*, and the rest of the students in the same class or who pursue the same science are the *opponents*, who are appointed to dispute or raise objections against the proposition affirmed or denied. It is the business of the respondent to write a thesis in Latin, or short discourse on the question proposed, and he either affirms or denies the question according to the opinion of the tutor, which is supposed to be the truth, and he reads it at the beginning of the dispute. The opponent, or opponents in succession, make objections in the form of a syllogism, the proposition in which is in reply argued against and denied by the respondent. During this time the tutor sits in the chair as President or Moderator to see that the rules of disputation and decency be observed on both sides. His work is also to illustrate and explain the answer or distinction of the respondent where it is obscure, to strengthen it where it is weak, and to correct it where it is false, and when the respondent is pinched with a strong objection, and is at a loss for an answer, the Moderator assists him and suggests some answer to the objection of the opponent, in defence of the question, according to his own opinion or sentiment."

The latter part of the above quotation seems to be the only ground for attributing an authorship to the præses, viz., that he has had so great a hand in correcting and moulding the form and argument of the essay as to be entitled to the appellation. I cannot understand the thesis being attributed to the præses on any other supposition, but if that supposition be correct, and the præses did give the candidate the information on which his dissertation is compiled, and the candidate had merely the superficial reality of the position as a defender of the statements given in his thesis, would not that circumstance be purely a literary question and a matter for a statement by foot-note ? while, as the candidate for honours brings the thesis forward as his own, he must bibliographically be considered its author.

The questions also arise : is the published thesis the original thesis prepared for disputation, or is it in its printed form a combination of that thesis with such corrections and emendations as have been elicited in the discussion ? Is it like a paper contributed to our societies, in which the *ipsissima verba* of the author are retained if the paper is thought generally worthy of publication, in despite of some of its statements having been contravened in the discussion ? Is it like a drafted Bill for Parliament, or as amended in committee or by a rival committee, with the chairman's notes of addition and correction? Might not the authorship, if conceded to the præses on these grounds, be given also to a schoolmaster who suggested some of the principal points of the themes for his pupils on which they were to gain honour and distinction; or to a drawing-master, who

"In years gone by, when we were lads at school,"

put some last brilliant touches to our dull, spiritless attempts at imitation; rendering our pencillings liable, in their improved condition, to be declared by some cynical critic, much to our dissatisfaction, more our master's than our own?

In the *Dissertationes Inaugurales* of the Edinburgh, Leipzig, Goettingen, Berlin, Paris, and other universities, there is little or no difficulty, where the author, A. B. *eruditorum examini subjicit, ex auctoritate Rectoris vel Præfecti,* as, if we take, for instance, the case of the Edinburgh Dissertations, no one could suppose the hundreds of dissertations submitted for examination by aspirants for academic honours could all be attributed, either

to the learned Præfects Drs. Wishart or
Wm. Robertson of the last century, or to
Dr. Georgius Baird of the first quarter of
the present; and one of the difficulties
connected with the question is, how far
the usual præses in thesis with a respondent, is or is not in almost the same
relative position as the rector of the above
dissertations, and in fact whether the
hundred and one different forms and
variations of words on title-pages used in
the various cases of rector and candidate
for honours, præses and proponent, præses
and defendant, defendant alone, præses
and respondent, respondent alone, etc.,
are not all slightly varying representations
of much the same condition of things,
modified perhaps by some variety of
usages, as in Sweden, for instance, which
may have been more favourable to the
claims of the præses than in other countries; a condition, however, which is a
veritable Proteus in its many changes of
shape.

Presidents, we allow to be absolute in
their decisions, but in the case of these
dissertations they are in an " ablative

absolute" position, and therefore, I suggest, should, with few exceptions, be removed from the status of author, which belongs grammatically as well as bibliographically to the proponent, defendant, or respondent, who in the nominative case dominates the entire construction of the title-page.

The British Museum rule, as adopted by Mr. Cutter in his *Rules for a Dictionary Catalogue* and by our Association since, viz., "*Consider the Respondent or Defendant of a Thesis as its Author except when it unequivocally appears to be the work of the Præses,*" does not comprehend cases where both the words respondent and defendant occur together.

The respondent is the author when words like *auctor respondens* are attached to his name, or when the præses is the only other name mentioned on the title, but not when there is a proponent or defendant, as in the following out of many instances I could produce :—

"*De Mangano :* Dissertatio quam publice *defendere* studebit G. Forchhammer, *respondente* Tho. G. Repp ;" Hafniæ, 1820, 4to. "Dissertatio Medica quam auspiciis

Rectoris Friderici Hassiæ Landgravii *defendet* P. J. Borellus, *respondente* H. G. Sibeckero."

I should like, therefore, to have added to that rule, "the Defendant or Respondent is the Author when either occurs separately on the title-page, but when together, the Defendant must be so considered."

In Cutter's rules for cross-referencing, he considers that one should be made from the præses to the respondent or defendant of a thesis, which I cannot but consider supererogatory; the contrary one, from respondent to præses, where the præses can be proved to be the author, has more reason in its favour.

This latter case is, however, of comparatively rare occurrence, the following being examples of those few cases in which the authorship must be given to him :—

"*Dissertatio quam sistit præses G. F. Francus de Frankenau, respondente Daniel Wagnero* ;" Hafniæ, 1704, the dedication being also signed by Francus. "*De Hu. moribus disputatio, authore ac præside D.*

8

C. Lucio et respondente M. Rotmundo,"
Ingolstadii, 1588.

In what way, favourable or unfavourable to the præses-author hypothesis, shall we take such titles as—

Deo triuno præside ex decreto gratiosi Med. Ordinis.

Quam deo ter optimo maximo Præside ex auctoritate D. Rectoris exam. subjicit J. G. W.

Quam præside summo numine ex auctoritate D. Rectoris subjicit J. G. W.

When the præses is the author he is usually called author, defendant, or proponent, never respondent, but the opposing respondent is sometimes a participating author.

The following case is one of our difficulties, and shows the necessity of looking further than the title :—

" *Dissertatio de Hæmorrhoidibus, præses Geo. Francus, respondens J. G. Carisius,* Heidelb. 1672."

The dedication to this is signed by Francus, with this remark, "*Dissertationem Medicam primitias nempe meas offerre debui,*" proving him to be the author.

And in numerous cases where the names of a præses and respondent occur on the title without the word author being attached to either, the preface or dedication is signed sometimes by one and sometimes by the other, and the authorship must be attributed accordingly.

But with regard to those Disputations in which only the names of præses and respondent occur on the title, we must recollect that the antithesis is not always between *them*, but between the *opponents*, whether mentioned or not, and the *author* who responds to their strictures, the præses being only the arbiter between them.

The principal cause of our troubles in these matters is not, however, to be found so much in the separate dissertations in their original publication, as in the collected editions of them by Haller and others. In these collections the name of the præses is constantly given as author of the thesis in the heading lines of the text, even when the title, in agreement with its original publication, attaches the word *auctor* to the name of the defendant or respondent ; are we in these cases to suppose that these heading lines have really been left to the caprice of the printer, who has adopted the name of the præses as occurring first on the title, on the principle of first come first served ?

In Haller's Collection of *Disputationes Chirurgicæ* contrarieties constantly occur, the exact sameness of construction in the titles being followed sometimes by the name of the præses and sometimes by that of the defendant, on the heading lines of the text ; as, for instance, in one where, though the fly-title mentions Orth as the "*respondens auctor,*" the dissertation is in the heading placed under the name of Salzmann, the præses.

Other instances of this difficulty occur in Gruner's *Delectus Dissertationum Medicarum Jenensium,* in which a large number are attributed to the præses Baldinger, in a title-construction which mentions the names of the proponents as authors. In Haller's *Disputationes ad Morborum historiam,* the regular titles are omitted, and the two names, sometimes præses and respondent, sometimes respondent and opponent, or defendant

and respondent, are given coupled by an
et as the authors of the dissertation, the
first name, however, gaining the honour of
the heading line. I give one or two instances exhibiting the confusion involved
in the question.

*J. V. Scheid et Marci Mappi Disputatio
de duobus ossiculis in cerebro humano mu-
lieris,* 1687. Scheid's name appears as the
author in the heading line, but on turning
to the original edition I find *pro disputa-
tione proposita, præside J. V. Scheid, respondente Marco Mappo,* and in the dedication
signed by Mappus it is stated by him
to be his first specimen of his medical
studies.

In another instance of the same kind,
*Joh. Saltzmann et E. C. Honold de Verme
naribus excusso,* the heading line has Saltzmann as the author, while in the original
edition the dedication to the magistracy
of his native town is signed by Honold,
as dedicating to them *primitias hasce aca-
demicas,* and at the end are several letters
and sets of congratulatory verses on his
performance. How in a bibliographical
sense can Scheid or Saltzmann be the

authors of these theses ? The information
they may have contributed as teachers
does not constitute them authors. Cases
of the same kind occur in *Richteri Opuscula Medica, studio J. C. G. Ackermann,*
1780; in *Trilleri Opuscula,* and in *J.
G. Roedereri Opuscula Medica,* in which
latter are included dissertations which are
said to be *totæ ab illo factæ,* which yet on
their titles have *quam publico eruditorum
examini submittit*—Dietz, Winiker, Hirsch-
feld, Stein, Schael, Chüden, Zeis, and some
with the word *auctor* prefixed to the proponent, and without the name of Roederer
on the title at all, which yet are said in the
table of contents to be *illo non plane auc-
tore sed suasore et moderatore enatæ.*

There is a series of thirteen *Disputationes de recta ratione Purgandi, a Mel-
chiore Sebizio,* 1621, which are printed as
by Sebizius, but in each of the disputations the dedication is signed by the
respondent, and the respondents speak of
the theses as the firstfruits of their studies.

There are, indeed, so many of these
dissertations in which the construction of
the title is the same whether a præses is

mentioned or not, and with the word auctor sometimes following the name of the defendant, sometimes that of the respondent, that there can be little doubt that one of the latter must be considered the author, in all cases where auctor does not follow the name of the præses.

When a collection of theses or dissertations is published under the name of a præses as his *opera*, such as in the case of Sebizius, Richter, Roederer, and others, it is merely in a secondary sense from his having contributed opinions and corrections to them ; and may there not also, in this publication of sets of theses under the name of the præses as his works, be some little display of bibliopolic art, as insuring a better sale if the name of an important professor of the place be attached to them than with those of yet obscure students bringing forth their first displays of knowledge before the academic world ?

And though I feel great objections to their being considered as authors bibliographically speaking, yet with regard to Linnæus, Thunberg, and some other Swedish authors, they really seem to have had so very much to do with the composition of the theses, at the disputations on which they sat as presidents, that I feel great difficulty in comprehending them in the previous category.

From these collections of dissertations it seems impossible to form any bibliographical conclusions as a basis for certainty of arrangement, but I will add from the previous statements a few suggestions which may tend towards that end :—

That the proponent is always the author of a dissertation.

That the defendant is always the author of a dissertation when it occurs with another name as respondent.

That the term defendant is, when alone, synonymous with respondent.

That when the respondent's name occurs with a præses only, the respondent is the author except words are attached to the president's name affirming him to be the proponent, defendant, or author, or there is evidence in the preface or dedication that he claims the authorship.

That the respondent when he is the

author is frequently described as auctor respondens.

That the opponent is never the author of a thesis.

That dissertatio, disputatio, thesis, etc., are generally used synonymously, the same construction of words as to the authorship following each.

And that when a collection of theses or dissertations is published under the name of a præses as his " opera " it is merely in a secondary literary sense, viz., his having contributed opinions and corrections to the theses, or as being their editor.

That the adoption of an asterisk in catalogues to denote an academical dissertation or thesis relieves us of the necessity of repeating a large amount of redundant wording to each title. It has been used successfully in the library of the Royal Medical and Chirurgical Society, and by Dr. Billings in his most valuable *Index-Catalogue of the Library of the Surgeon-General's Office, United States.*

HEADINGS OTHER THAN AUTHOR
HEADINGS.

Reports of trials are frequently difficult
to catalogue, and some persons who are
anxious to find an author for a book have
considered the reporter as such. This I
consider a hopeless mistake, for the name
of the reporter is little likely to be retained
in the memory of the searcher, who is
sure to remember the subject of the trial.
Mr. Cutter's remark upon this point is
very just. He says : " It may be doubted
. . . whether a stenographic reporter is
entitled to be considered an author any
more than a type-setter."

The British Museum rule is as follows :—

" XXXVII. Reports of civil actions to
be catalogued under the name of that
party to the suit which stands first upon
the title-page.

" In criminal proceedings the name of
the defendant to be adopted as a heading.

" Trials relating to any vessel to be
entered under the name of such vessel."

Mr. Cutter adopts this rule, but he
simplifies the wording. His rule is :—

" 48. Trials may be entered only under

the name of the defendant in a criminal suit and the plaintiff in a civil suit, and trials relating to vessels under the name of the vessel."

The treatment of catalogues in a catalogue has given rise to a considerable amount of difference of opinion. The British Museum rules on this subject appear to meet the difficulties clearly and well.

" LXXXV. Anonymous catalogues, whether bearing the title 'catalogue' or any other intended to convey the same meaning, to be entered under the head 'Catalogues,' subdivided as follows :—

" 1st. Catalogues of public establishments (including those of societies, although not strictly speaking *public*). 2nd. Catalogues of private collections, drawn up either for sale or otherwise. 3rd. Catalogues of collections not for sale, the possessors of which are not known. 4th. General as well as special catalogues of objects without any reference to their possessor. 5th. Dealers' catalogues. 6th. Sale catalogues not included in any of the preceding sections."

In the foregoing rule the word " anonymous " would, I think, be better omitted.
It seems absurd to omit under the heading
such catalogues as may happen to have
the name of the compiler on the title-
page.   He is in no proper sense the
author.   Of course there are some books
in which the word " catalogue " is used that
should come under the names of the
authors.   This rule applies only to catalogues of particular collections, and not
to such books as *Catalogue of Works of
Velasquez in the Galleries of Europe*,
which should be placed under the name
of its compiler, who is as much its author
as he is of *The Life of Velasquez*.

The Cambridge rule is as follows :—

" Catalogues of all descriptions to be
entered under the superior heading CATA-
LOGUE, to be followed, in the case of all
other articles than books, by the word or
phrase (used in the title) which expresses
what they are, printed in italics.   The
word CATALOGUE standing alone, to be
used for catalogues of books, whether of
private libraries, booksellers, or auctions,
In the case of institutions, the name of

the town and institution to be subjoined
in italics to the word ' catalogue ' in the
superior heading. In the title which
follows the superior heading, preference
to be given to the owner rather than the
compiler, in choosing a leading word for
the entry."

The Library Association rule is :—

" Catalogues are to be entered under
the name of the institution, or owner of
the collection, with a cross-reference from
the compiler."

Mr. Cutter is opposed to the plan
adopted in the above rules. He says :—

" 8. Booksellers and auctioneers are to
be considered as the authors of their
catalogues unless the contrary is expressly
asserted. Entering these only under the
form-heading CATALOGUES belongs to the
dark ages of cataloguing. Put the catalogue of a library under the library's
name."

I cannot understand why a system of
arranging catalogues under a general
heading, where they are most likely to
be sought for, should be stigmatized as
belonging to the dark ages. It is im-

possible to imagine a worse heading for
an auction catalogue than the name of
the auctioneer. His name is seldom
quoted, and more often forgotten. By
this rule, unless a special exception is
introduced, the Heber Catalogue would
be separated under the names of Evans,
Sotheby, and Wheatley.

It is necessary to bear in mind that
catalogues are not really books, and to
make them follow rules adapted for true
books is only confusing, and leads to no
useful end. One great advantage of
bringing them under the heading of
" Catalogues " is that they can be tabulated
and the titles condensed. It becomes
needless to repeat such formulæ as "to
be sold by auction," or "forming the
stock of," etc.

The title of a true book is an individual
entity, the outcome of an author's mind ;
but this is not the case with a catalogue.
Its title, like that of a journal or publication
of a society, is formed upon a system.

It will be seen that the Cambridge
rule improves upon that of the British
Museum in respect to arrangement. By

the latter, catalogues of books, coins, estates, and botanical specimens are mixed up together. These should each be arranged separately.

Concordances are usually placed under the headings of the works to which they relate. The compiler of a concordance must not, however, be overlooked, and it is necessary to make a reference to his name. In some instances, such as Cruden's *Concordance*, the user of the catalogue is more likely to look under "Cruden" than under " Bible." All the best authorities group together under the heading of BIBLE the Old and New Testaments and their separate parts. Also commentaries, etc.

Another important heading is that of *Liturgies*, which is likely to be extensive in a large public library. It requires the special arrangement of an expert, but the British Museum and the Cambridge University rules deal with this subject.

There is some difficulty in choosing the proper heading for certain reports of voyages. Sometimes these are written by an author whose name occurs on the title-page. In these instances the book is naturally catalogued under its author's name, and it is only necessary to make a reference under the name of the vessel.

But there is another class of voyages more elaborate in their arrangement, which either are anonymous or have many authors. There is usually an account of the voyage, and then a series of volumes devoted to zoology, botany, etc. Sometimes these voyages are catalogued under the name of the commander as Dumont d'Urville for *Voyage autour du Monde de la Corvette l'Astrolabe ;* but it is in every way more convenient to use the name of the vessel as a heading, and bring all the different divisions under it, as *Astrolabe, Challenger,* etc.

ANONYMOUS AND PSEUDONYMOUS WORKS.

We now· come to consider the large question of the treatment of anonymous books. I read a paper on this subject at the Conference of Librarians, and I venture to transfer to these pages the substance of that paper with some further remarks. Before entering into the discussion I wish to protest against the use of the term "anonym," which appears to me to be formed upon a false analogy. It may be a convenient word, but it is incorrect. A pseudonym is an entity—a false name under cover of which an author chooses to write; but an anonymous book has a title from which an important something is omitted, viz., the author's name. You cannot express a negation such as this by a distinctive term like "anonym." I am sorry to see that the term has found a place in the Philological Society's *New English Dictionary* (Murray), although it is stated to be of rare occurrence in this sense.

In dealing with the titles of anonymous books, it is necessary, in the first place, to agree upon the definition of an anonymous book. Barbier, who published the first edition of his useful *Dictionnaire des Ouvrages Anonymes et Pseudonymes* in 1806, gives the following: "On appelle ouvrage anonyme celui sur le frontispice duquel l'auteur n'est pas nommé."

Mr. Cutter gives the same definition, and adds : " Strictly, a book is not anonymous if the author's name appears anywhere in it, but it is safest to treat it as anonymous if the author's name does not appear in the title."

The Bodleian rule (16) also is :—" If the name of a writer occur in a work, but not on the title-page, the work is also to be regarded for the purpose of headings as anonymous, except in the case of works without separate title-page."

Barbier, however, in the second edition of his book (1822), was forced by the vastness of his materials to adopt a more rigid rule. The best definition of an anonymous work would probably take something of this form : A book printed without the author's name, either in the title or in the preliminary matter.

According to the British Museum rule, a book which has been published without the author's name always remains anonymous, even after the author is well known and the book has been republished with the name on the title-page. By this means you have the same book in two places. For instance, the anonymous editions of *Waverley* are catalogued under "Waverley," and the others under "Scott." But for cataloguing purposes a book surely ceases to be anonymous when the author's name is known. We ought never to lose sight of the main object of a catalogue, which is to help the consulter, and not to present him with a series of bibliographical riddles. If we settle that all anonymous works shall be entered under the authors' names when known, the question has still to be answered, What is to be done with those which remain unknown? Some cataloguers have objected to the insertion of subject-headings in the same alphabet with authors' names, and in the old catalogue of the Royal Society Library the plan was adopted of placing all anonymous titles under the useless heading of " Anonymous."

The British Museum rule 38 directs that in the case of all anonymous books not arranged under proper names according to previous rules, the first substantive in the title (or if there be no substantive, the first word) shall be selected as the heading. " A substantive adjectively used, to be taken in conjunction with its following substantive as forming one word, and the same to be done with respect to adjectives incorporated with their following substantive."

The great objection to this rule is that an important word in a title may throw very little light upon the subject of the book. Mr. Cutter's rule is : " Make a first-word entry for all anonymous works except anonymous biographies, which are to be entered under the name of the subject of the life." When this rule is applied, the majority of books will be placed under headings for which no one is likely to seek, so that many cross-references will be necessary. For instance, *A True and Exact Account of the Scarlet Gowns* is entered under " True," which we may safely say would be the last word looked for. It is these redundant words of a title-page that are pretty sure to escape the memory. All the rules that I have seen relating to anonymous books appear to me to be based upon a fundamental confusion of the essential differences between a catalogue and a bibliography. When Barbier compiled his valuable work, he adopted the simple plan of arranging each title under the first word not an article, which works admirably, because the consulter has the book whose author he seeks in his hand. In the case of a catalogue it is quite different, for the consulter has not the book before him, and wishes to find it from the leading idea of the title, which is probably all he remembers.

The rule I would propose is, to take as a heading the word which best explains the objects of the author, in whatever part of the title it may be. The objection that may be raised to this is that it is not rigid enough; but the cataloguer should be allowed a certain latitude, and it is well that the maker of the catalogue should try to place himself in the position of the user of it in these cases.[1]

[1] "On the Alphabetical Arrangement of the Titles of Anonymous Books" (*Transactions and Proceedings of the Conference of Librarians,* 1877, pp. 97-9).

The Bodleian rule (16) is good :—
" Under the first striking word or words
of the titles of anonymous works with a
second heading or cross reference, when
advisable under or from any other notice-
able word or catch-title."

The evidence before the Commission
of 1847-49 contains much opinion about
the treatment of anonymous works in
the Catalogue of the British Museum.
The general feeling of the witnesses was
adverse to the system, but Sir Anthony
Panizzi argued strongly in favour of his
plan. The plan actually adopted was
not to Panizzi's taste, and doubtless the
changes which were introduced caused
some confusion. The Commissioners
reported on this subject as follows :—

" To another instance in which Mr.
Panizzi's opinion was overruled by that
of the Trustees he attributes much avoid-
able delay and expense ; we allude to
the 33rd and seven following rules, which
govern the process of cataloguing anonymous works. It will appear from the
evidence, that some of our principal
witnesses are at issue on questions

involved in the consideration of this subject. It seems clear enough that no one rule can be adopted which will not lead to instances apparently anomalous and absurd. Such authorities, however, as Mr. Maitland and Professor De Morgan, are nevertheless of opinion, that some one rule should be devised and strictly observed, while Mr. Collier and others are of opinion that free scope may be left to the discretion of the parties employed. Mr. Panizzi having to deal with an immense mass of works under this head, advocates the adoption and the rigid observance of a rule by which the main entries of all such works should find their places in the Catalogue in alphabetical order, under the first word of the title not an article or preposition. To certain decisions of the Trustees which have compelled him to depart from this rule, he attributes many defects in the work already executed, and, above all, much of that delay so loudly complained of in its progress."

Panizzi's arguments quite converted the Commissioners, and they added to

their statement of the case these words :
" We recommend for the future that
Mr. Panizzi should be released from an
observance of these rules, and directed
to proceed, with regard to anonymous
works, upon such system as under present
circumstances may appear to him best
calculated to reconcile the acceleration of
the work with its satisfactory execution."

Mr. Parry in his evidence made some
remarks on this subject. He said :—
" If Mr. Panizzi's plan, with respect to
anonymous works, had been adopted,
it would have given great facility to the
compilation of the Catalogue ; his plan
was the plan of Audiffredi, in the Catalogue of the Casanate Library at Rome,
and the plan followed by Barbier in his
Dictionnaire des Anonymes ; [1] that plan
was taking the first word, not an article
or preposition, or, as it might be modified, the first substantive, for the heading
of the title. I am quite aware that the

[1] Referring to my remarks on the use of the
word " anonym," I may point out that this is
not the correct title of Barbier's work. He
used *Anonymes* as an adjective (*ouvrages anonymes*), and not as a substantive.

plan seems almost absurd upon the face of it. For example, supposing there was such a title as this, *The Lame Duck; or, A Rumour from the Stock Exchange,* why, that would come under 'Lame' or 'Duck,' according to that plan; but if that plan be taken in conjunction with an index of matters, whilst it would materially facilitate the formation of a catalogue, it would cease to be objectionable. I believe one of the great hindrances being anonymous works,—there have been more difficulties and more labour about anonymous works than about any other portion of the Catalogue,—the plan suggested by Mr. Panizzi originally, and which he would have adopted, but which the trustees objected to, taken in conjunction with the index of matters at the end, is by no means an absurd plan " (p. 469).

Sir Frederick Madden, when under examination, said : "The first point in the statement I wish to make is with reference to the cataloguing of anonymous works; that the plan adopted is founded altogether upon a mistaken notion, so much so that

I should say in nine cases out of ten the books cannot be found. I cannot understand upon what principle it is that a book is to be entered by the first substantive or the first word rather than the last. It seems to me that the principle is entirely fallacious." I entirely agree with Sir F. Madden, and I can speak from bitter experience of the great difficulty there is in finding anonymous books in the British Museum Catalogue.

Lord Mahon (afterwards Earl Stanhope), one of the trustees, dealt with this matter very satisfactorily in his examination. He said :—

"I will take the heading 'Account' as I find it in the *Catalogue of the Letter A*, printed in 1841. Under that heading I find seventeen entries of different books, and I am of opinion with respect to all the seventeen that the heading 'Account' is one of the least convenient under which they could stand. The entries are such as these :—

> *An Account of Several Workhouses for Employing and Maintaining the Poor.* London, 1725. 4°.

An Account of the Constitution and Security of the General Bank of Credit. London, 1683. 4°.

An Exact Account of Two Real Dreams which happened to the Same Person. London, 1725. 8.

An Impartial Account of the Prophets, in a Letter to a Friend. Edinburgh. 4°.

An Account of the Proceedings in Order to the Discovery of the Longitude. London, 1765. 4°.

It seems to me, that these works could be entered far more conveniently under the headings respectively of 'Workhouses,' 'Banks,' 'Dreams,' 'Prophets,' and 'Longitude.' Now, to take only the last case, the book upon the longitude, it should be considered that probably a reader would only be directed to that book through one of two channels. In the first place, he might desire, by means of the Catalogue, to have an opportunity of examining all the publications that have appeared on the subject of the longitude; and if he do not find these publications collected under the heading 'Longitude,' in what a labyrinth of perquisitions must he become involved![1] Or, secondly, he may have seen the book in question referred to by some other writer on science. But in such a case the reference is seldom given at full length; it is far more commonly comprised in some such words as the following : " The proceedings to discover the longitude up to 1763 are well described in an anonymous tract published in the same year ;' or, 'An essay, without the author's name, published in 1763, gives a good summary of the proceedings so far towards the discovery of the longitude ;' or again, 'For these facts, see the *Proceedings towards the Discovery of the Longitude* (London, 1763).' Now with such a reference, if the book in question had been entered under ' Longitude,' it would be found readily and at once ; but if not, how is the inquirer to know that he should seek it under 'Account' rather than under 'Essay,' 'Treatise,' 'Dissertation,' 'Remarks,' 'Observations,' 'Letter,'

---

[1] This point weakens Lord Mahon's arguments, because the same objection would apply to all the books with authors' names.

'History,' 'Narrative,' 'Statement,' or any other similar heading?" (p. 812).

Mr. C. Tomlinson referred in his evidence to the effects of rule XXXIV., by which the name of a country is adopted as a heading. He instanced the anonymous work (known, however, to have been written by John Holland) entitled, *The History and Description of Fossil Fuel ; the Collieries and Coal Trade of Great Britain.* He says : " This book has occasioned me a great deal of search. I looked under the head of 'Coal,' I looked under 'Collieries,' and I looked under 'Fuel,' and it is not to be found under any of those titles, but it is found under ' Great Britain and Ireland'" (p. 305).

Mr. Panizzi alludes to this in his reply to criticisms. He says that under his own rule it would appear under "History," but under the system of taking the main subject it properly comes under "Great Britain" (p. 677).

Mr. John Bruce objected to *L'Art de Vérifier les Dates, The Art of Cookery,* and *The Art of Love* all coming under the heading of "Art," and here I should agree with him; but when he proceeded to suggest that a book entitled, *Is it Well with You?* should be entered under "Well" because that is the emphatic word (p. 423), I think he is wrong. This is a distinctive title similar to the title of a novel, and likely to be completely quoted and to remain on the memory, and therefore the book should be entered under "Is."

I hope enough has been said to show that the system adopted by Mr. Panizzi, however clear and logical, is not a convenient one for the person who wishes to discover the title of an anonymous book in the catalogue.

There seem to have been two reasons for adopting this system: first, that it was simple; and, secondly, that the other plan of putting a title under a subject-heading was confusing classification with alphabetization. Lord Wrottesley put this point as a question: "Any other system of cataloguing anonymous works than the system which you recommend does in point of fact confound two different things, a classed catalogue and an alphabetical catalogue ? " To which Mr. Panizzi answered, " Yes."

With respect to the first reason, I allow that the rule is simple, and can be rigidly followed by a staff of cataloguers, but a catalogue is not made for the convenience of the cataloguer. It is intended for the convenience of the consulter ; and if the titles are placed under headings for which the consulter is not likely to look, the system signally fails in this respect.

With respect to the second reason, I do not see that the only alternative to the use of the first substantive or first important word is classification. And, further, referring to the work on fossil fuel lately alluded to, is it not as much a classification to make the heading " Great Britain " as to make it "Coal" or " Fuel " ?

The great object should be, not to classify, but to choose as a heading the word which is likely to remain in the memory, instead of one which is as likely to escape it.

To give an instance of what I mean. Suppose we had to catalogue a publication issued during the course of the

Crimean War, entitled, *Whom shall we Hang?* This I should put under " W," and not under the Crimean War, because the whole of this sentence is likely to remain in the memory. Again, in a foreign title, I should take the prominent word as it stands on the title, and not translate it. It is the title of the book that we have to deal with, and not the subject of it.

In cataloguing a library, I think the only safe way is to keep all the anonymous titles together to the last, and then make headings for them at the same time and upon one system. Errors are likely to occur if the heading is finally made when the book is first catalogued, and such errors have crept into the British Museum, as may be seen from the following extracts :—

Champions, Seven Champions of Christendom. See " Seven Champions."
Seven Champions of Christendom. See " Christendom."
Christendom, Seven Champions of. See " Seven Champions of."

I have not noticed that much remark

has been made on rule XXXII., by which
" works published under initials [are] to
be entered under the last of them ; " but
I think it is one of the most successful modes of hiding away titles under a
heading least likely to be remembered.
When titles are quoted pretty fully and
accurately, it is seldom that the initials on
a title are quoted ; and if these initials are
only at the end of the preface, they are
never likely to be remembered. Thus by
placing the title in the catalogue under
the initials (in whatever order they may
be taken), it is buried entirely out of sight,
and is practically useless. The Rev. Dr.
Biber remarked upon this point in his
evidence. He said : " The remarks which
I made about letter A were merely made
incidentally, because, having noticed the
difficulty of finding books which were
catalogued under initials, I wished to satisfy
myself as to what arrangement there was "
(p. 577).

I presume that this arrangement under
initials has been found inconvenient at
the British Museum, because in the
useful *Explanation of the System of the*

Catalogue I find a note as to special cross-references, which are to be made to " works under initials from whatever heading the work would have been entered under, but for the initials." We are informed, however, that " at present this has not been fully carried out."

Another point connected with this class of books is one of particular difficulty. I refer to the treatment of pseudonyms, which are dealt with in rules XLI., XLII., and XLIII. :—

"XLI. In the case of pseudonymous publications, the book to be catalogued under the author's feigned name ; and his real name, if discovered, to be inserted in brackets, immediately after the feigned name, preceded by the letters '*i.e.*'

"XLII. Assumed names, or names used to designate an office, profession, party, or qualification of the writer, to be treated as real names. Academical names to follow the same rule. The works of an author not assuming any name, but describing himself by a circumlocution, to be considered anonymous.

"XLIII. Works falsely attributed in

their title to a particular person, to be treated as pseudonymous."

There is much to be said for this arrangement under pseudonyms, but there is also much to be said against it. In the first place, an author may, and often does, take in the course of his literary life several pseudonyms, which are merely adopted for a temporary purpose, and thus the works of the same author will be spread about in several parts of the alphabet. There does not appear to be any particular advantage in separating Sir Walter Scott's works under such headings as "Jedediah Cleishbotham" and "Malachi Malagrowther." Sometimes, also, these pseudonyms are so unlike real names that they are passed by unquoted, and the same difficulty occurs as in the case of initials.

When, however, an author takes a name under which he always writes, and by which he is always known, it seems scarcely worth while to put the author's works under a practically unknown name, instead of under a well-known one. This, however, does not often occur in the case of an author, although it frequently does in the case of an authoress. For instance, George Eliot has written her name in literature, and is always known by that name, so that to place her works under Evans or Lewes or Crosse is to change the known for the unknown. In a lesser degree this is the case with the novelist known as Sarah Tytler, whose real name is Henrietta Keddie. Probably not one in a thousand of her readers knows this fact.

Mr. Cutter makes some very pertinent remarks upon this point. His note to his rule 5, "Enter pseudonymous works under the author's real name, when it is known, with a reference from the pseudonym," is as follows :—

"One is strongly tempted to deviate from this rule in the case of writers like George Eliot and George Sand, Gavarni and Grandville, who appear in literature only under their pseudonyms. It would apparently be much more convenient to enter their works under the name by which they are known, and under which everybody but a professed cataloguer would assuredly look first. For an author-catalogue this might be the best plan, but in a dictionary catalogue we have to deal with such people not merely as writers of books, but as subjects of biographies or parties in trials, and in such cases it seems proper to use their legal names. Besides, if one attempts to exempt a few noted writers from the rule given above, where is the line to be drawn? No definite principle of exception can be laid down which will guide either the cataloguer or the reader; and probably the confusion would in the end produce greater inconvenience than the present rule. Moreover the entries made by using the pseudonym as a heading would often have to be altered. For a long time it would have been proper to enter the works of Dickens under Boz; the Dutch annual bibliography uniformly use "Boz-Dickens" as a heading. No one would think of looking under Boz now. Mark Twain is in a transition state. The public mind is divided between Twain and Clemens. The tendency is always towards the use of the real name; and that tendency will be much helped in the reading public if the real name is always preferred in catalogues. Some pseudonyms persistently adopted by authors have come to be considered as the only names, as Voltaire, and the translation Melanchthon. Perhaps George Sand and George Eliot will in time be adjudged to belong to the same company. It would be well if cataloguers could appoint some permanent committee with authority to decide this and similar points as from time to time they occur."

If the French bibliographer had borne in mind the British Museum rule, that " the works of an author not assuming any name, but describing himself by a circumlocution [are] to be considered anonymous," he would not have made this amusing entry in his catalogue : " *Herself,* Memoirs of a Young Lady by."

The Cambridge rules were largely founded upon those of the British Museum, and many anomalies crept into the catalogue on account of the difficulties caused by the rules relating to anonymous works ; but a few years before the lamented death of Mr. Henry Bradshaw[1] these rules were considerably altered by him, and I think the statement in rules 28 and 29 as they now stand is by far the most satisfactory of any I know of :—

" 28. Anonymous works which refer to neither person nor place, and to which none of the foregoing rules can be applied, to be catalogued under the name of the subject (whether a single word or a composite phrase) which is prominently referred to on the title-page ; the primary consideration being, under what heading the book will be most easily found. When there is no special subject mentioned, and the title is a catch-title (as in the case of most novels and many pamphlets), the first word not an article to stand at the head in capitals, but not to be separated off from the title as a heading. When the indication on the title is insufficient, the heading understood to be taken, but all classification to be avoided, the words of the title being exclusively used as far

[1] I had the privilege of talking over these rules with Mr. Bradshaw for many consecutive days, when I inspected the University Library in 1878.

as possible. Works to be catalogued under general headings only where such are unavoidable. In the case of foreign titles the heading to follow the same rule, and to be in the language of the title instead of being translated.

" 29. When the author of a pseudonymous or anonymous work is ascertained and acknowledged after the title has been printed, the name to be added within a bracket at the end of the title; and the various titles of works thenceforward assigned to such author to be gathered under his name by means of written entries on the slips. Cross-references to be printed from the pseudonymous or anonymous heading to the author's name."

These remarks upon the cataloguing of anonymous works may appear to some to have run to an inordinate length, but the great importance of the subject will, I hope, be accepted by the reader as some excuse. I quite agree with the late Serjeant Parry when he said, during his examination before the British Museum Commission, that "it is comparatively easy to catalogue when the author's name appears on the title, but nothing is more difficult than cataloguing anonymous works."

THE TITLE.

Having dealt with the subject of headings, we may now pass on to consider the treatment of the title itself.

There has been much discussion on this subject : one party has been in favour of short titles, and another of long titles. Much has been said in favour of single-line catalogues, and these often form very useful keys to a library; but they are perhaps more properly designated alphabetical lists than catalogues.[1]

On the other side the advocates of full titles, in carrying out their views, while adding to the size of their catalogues, frequently do not add to their utility. Here, as in many other things, the medium is the safest way. The least important works have usually the longest

---

[1] For useful notes on short titles and booksellers' catalogues, Mr. Charles F. Blackburn's amusing *Hints on Catalogue Titles and on Index Entries* (1884) may be consulted.

titles, and it is surely useless to copy the whole title of some trumpery pamphlet, when it may occupy ten or a dozen lines of print. Here the art of the cataloguer comes into play, by which he is enabled to choose what is important and reject the redundant. With respect to standard works by classical authors, it is well to give the whole title (and these titles will seldom be found to be long). The classical author will most probably have weighed the words of his title with care, and left little that is redundant. When a title is contracted, it is well to insert dots to show that something has been left out, and if any words are added they must be placed between square brackets.

It is also necessary to bear in mind the fact that a long title may be perfectly clear in the book itself, on account of the varied size of the type used. The cataloguer, however, has not these facilities of arrangement at his disposal, and in consequence it becomes difficult for the consulter to distinguish the important parts of the title from the unimportant.

The following are three titles of books which are not long, and which could not be curtailed without disadvantage :—

" 1. Pike (Luke Owen). A History of Crime in England, illustrating the Changes of the Laws in the Progress of Civilization. Written from the Public Records and other Contemporary Evidence. London, 1873. 2 vols., 8vo.

" 2. Hunter (Joseph). New Illustrations of the Life, Studies, and Writings of Shakespeare ; Supplementary to all the Editions. London, 1845. 2 vols., 8vo.

" 3. Rickman (Thomas). An Attempt to Discriminate the Styles of Architecture in England, from the Conquest to the Reformation, with a Sketch of the Grecian and Roman Orders ; Seventh Edition, with Considerable Additions, Chiefly Historical, by John Henry Parker. Oxford, 1881. 8vo."

Now, we may take the instance of a long title, which needs curtailment :—

"The

English Expositor

Improv'd:

Being a Complete

Dictionary,

teaching

The Interpretation of the most Difficult Words, which are commonly made use of in our English Tongue.

First set forth by J. B., Doctor of Physick. And now carefully Revised, Corrected, and abundantly Augmented, with a new and very large Addition of very useful and significant Words.

By R. Browne, Author of the

English School Reform'd.

There is also an Index of Common Words (alphabetically set) to direct the Reader or others more Learned, and of the same signification with them. And likewise a short Nomenclator of the most celebrated Persons among the Ancients ; with Variety of Memorable Things : Collected out of the best of History, Poetry, Philosophy, and Geography.

The Twelfth Edition.

London : Printed for W. Churchill, at the Black Swan in Pater-noster-Row. 1719. Where may be had the above-mention'd Spelling-Book, Entituled, *The English School Reform'd :* Being a method very exact and easy both for the Teacher and Learner."

This long title may be reduced into the following form :—

"4. B[ullokar] (J[ohn]). The English Expositor Improv'd : Being a Complete Dictionary, teaching the Interpretation of the most Difficult Words, which are commonly made use of in our English Tongue. . . . Revised, Corrected, and . Augmented . . . by R. Browne, . . [with] an Index of Common Words . . . and . a short Nomenclator of the most Celebrated Persons among the Ancients, with Variety of Memorable Things. . . . 12th Edition.

London, 1719. 12mo."

It may be said that all these titles are in English, and present few difficulties. I therefore add a Latin title, prepared by my brother, the late Mr. B. R. Wheatley. The full title is as follows :—

"Spceulum Polytechnum Mathematicum novum,
tribus visionibus illustre
quarum extat

Una Funda–
mentalis Aliquot

Numerorum Danielis et Apo-

calypseos naturæ et proprie-
tatis Consignatio
Altera, usus Hactenus
incognitus Instrumenti Da-
-nielis Speccelii, ad altitudinum, profun-
-ditatum, longitudinum, latitudinumque dimen-
-siones, nec non Planimetricas delineationes
accommodatio.

Postrema brevis ac luculenta se-

-xies Acuminati Proportionum Cir-
-cini quibus fructuose iste adhibeatur
enarratio
In Omnium Mathesin Adamantium
Emolumentum
prius Germanicè æditum
Authore

Joanne Faulhabero Arithmetico

et Logista Ulmensi ingeniosissimo
Posterius vero ne tanto aliæ na-
-tiones defraudentur bono, Latine conversum
per

Joannem Remmelinum Ph. et Med.
Doctorem

Impressum Ulmæ, typis Joannis
Mederi
M.DC.XII."

This long title may be reduced into the following catalogue form :—

   " Faulhaber (Joannes).

   " Speculum Polytechnum Mathematicum novum tribus visionibus . . . una : . . . Numerorum Danielis et Apocalypseos naturæ . . . consignatio ; altera : usus. . . . Instrumenti Danielis Speccelii, ad altitudinum [etc.] dimensiones . . . accommodatio ; postrema : . . . sexies Acuminati Proportionum Circini . . . enarratio ; . . . prius Germanice æditum, . . . Latine conversum per Joannem Remmelinum. . . .

   Ulmæ, 1612. 4to."

Sometimes it is advisable to repeat the author's name in its proper place on the title either in full or with initials. This is the case with Dilke's *Papers of a Critic,* which should appear in the catalogue as follows :—

   " 6. Dilke (Charles Wentworth). The Papers of a Critic. Selected from the Writings of the late C. W. D., with a Biographical Sketch by his Grandson, Sir Charles Wentworth

Dilke, Bart., M.P.   London, 1875.
2 vols., 8vo."

Mr. Jewett, in his rules, directs that the position of the author's name on the title-page should be indicated.

For scarce and curious books it is under some circumstances useful to mark the position of the lines on a title-page thus :—

" 7. Bacon (Francis) Viscount St. Alban. | The | Essayes | or | Counsels | Civill and | Morall | of | Francis Lo. Verulam | Viscount St. Alban newly written | London | Printed by John Haviland for | Hanna Barret | 1625 | 4to."

This is clearly not necessary in the case of common modern books.

It is very important that all indication of edition or editor (as in No. 3) should be made clear on the catalogue slip ; and if this information is not given on the title-page, but can be obtained elsewhere, it should be added to the catalogue slip, but between square brackets.

Many books have two title-pages, an engraved one and a printed one, and these frequently differ in the wording. In these cases the printed title-page is the one to be followed. Sometimes a second title-page will occur in the middle of a book, and the cataloguer must be careful not to make two books out of one. When the contents of this second title-page are noted on the first title-page, it is not necessary to refer to it specially, unless a collation is given. If, however, this second title-page contain additional matter, it should be catalogued and added on the slip, but within parentheses, thus ( ), to show that it is added, and that it is not made up by the cataloguer, which would be understood if it were placed between square brackets, thus [ ].

Sometimes a title-page not only gives no real indication of the contents of a book, but is positively misleading. In such a case the cataloguer will do well to give some indication of the true contents, either in a note or as an addition to the title within brackets. Both Mr. Cutter and Professor Otis Robinson refer, in the *Special Report on Public Libraries in the United States,* to the difficulties caused by these misleading titles. Professor Robinson gives some amusing instances of modern clap-trap titles which may well be added to Disraeli's *Curiosities of Literature.*

"Mr. Parker writes a series of biographical sketches, and calls it *Morning Stars of the New World.* Somebody prepares seven religious essays, binds them up in a book, and calls it *Seven Stormy Sundays.* . . . An editor, at intervals of business, indulges his true poetic taste for the pleasure of his friends, or the entertainment of an occasional audience. Then his book appears, entitled, not *Miscellaneous Poems,* but *Asleep in the Sanctum,* by A. A. Hopkins. Sometimes, not satisfied with one enigma, another is added. Here we have *The Great Iron Wheel; or, Republicanism Backwards and Christianity Reversed,* by J. R. Graves."

In cataloguing books it is very important to turn carefully over the leaves to see that a second book, which may have been bound up in the volume, is not overlooked. It was a frequent practice at one time to bind up thin books with thicker ones, to save the expense of binding; and very frequently these thin additions are overlooked altogether, and never catalogued.

PLACE OF PUBLICATION.

When we have finished with the title proper, we come to consider the imprint, the date, and the size. These are most commonly arranged thus, volumes, size, place, date; and this is the best order if this information is tabulated; but when it remains as a part of the title, it is better to place the volumes and size at the end, because this is added information not found in the title-page.

The name of the place of publication [1] should be given exactly as it occurs on the title-page, and in old and rare books the name of the printer or publisher may be added with advantage; not necessarily full as it appears there, but shortened

---

[1] The names of places as they appear in a Latin form are frequently much disguised. A list of some of the most common of these names will be found in the Appendix.

and placed between parentheses. Sometimes several places are named on a title-page, but in these cases it is not necessary to notice more than the first.

DATES.

The dates, which usually occur in Roman numerals on the title-pages of books, should be printed in the catalogue with Arabic numerals, except in case of very rare books, where it is thought expedient to copy the original title-page exactly. Every one knows the numerical power of the letters, and that M stands for 1,000, D = 500, C = 100, L = 50, X = 10, V, U, = 5, I = 1; but the old printers were fond of playing tricks with the letters, and they allowed themselves much latitude in the practice of reducing the numerical power of one letter by placing another before it. We are used to this in IV and IX; but the following dates, copied from books, show how varied were the arrangements formerly made use of:—

MIID. = 1498, MID. = 1499, MCDXCIX. = 1499, MDXXCV. = 1585,

MDIC. = 1599, MDCVIV. = 1609, MIIDCC. = 1698.

In one book MVICXXI. was made to stand for 1621; but in this case the printer must have lacked a D, and replaced it by VI. In old books the M's and the D's are frequently built up thus, CIↃ, IↃ.

The date is one of the most important portions of a title, and the cataloguer must seek for it until he finds it. Sometimes it is to be found at the end of the preface or dedication, and sometimes it is on the title-page as a chronogram. Mr. James Hilton for years has searched over Europe for chronograms, and he has been highly successful in his search, as is evidenced by his two handsome volumes, *Chronograms, 5,000 and more in Number* (1882), and *Chronograms Continued and Concluded* (1885).

The following specimens are from Mr. Hilton's books :—

" Anagrammata regia in honorem maximi mansuetissimi regis Caroli conscripta."

Imprint :—

" LONDINI REGIO PRIVILEGIO EXARATVM = 1626."

On the last page is :—

"ᴇXᴛᴀɴᴛ Iꜱᴛᴀ Iɴ ÆDIʙVꜱ ɢVLIᴇLMI ꜱᴛᴀɴꜱʙIᴇ =
1626"

A curious little book (a chronographic imitation of Thomas à Kempis) is filled with chronograms, and contains two on the title-page :—

Dᴇ ꜱᴩIʀIᴛᴀLI IMIᴛᴀᴛIᴏɴᴇ CʜʀIꜱᴛI [1658]
ᴀDMᴏɴIᴛIᴏɴᴇꜱ ꜱᴀCʀᴁ ᴇᴛ VᴛILᴇꜱ [1658]
ᴩIIꜱ Iɴ LVCᴇM Dᴀᴛᴁ [1658]."

"a R.P. Antonio Vanden Stock Societatis Jesu.
Ruræmundæ apud Gasparem du Pree."

On the frontispiece is another chronogram :—

"chrIsto aDhærens non aMbVLat In tenebrIs."

Mr. Hilton has succeeded in finding several additions to the small store of chronograms in English, and has produced some new ones.

On the back of the title-page of the first book is this inscription :—

"An eXCeLLent neVV book of ChronograMs
gathereD together & noVV set forth by I.
ʜILton, F.S.A. = 1882."

On the second book :—

"Another qVIte neVV book of rIght eXCeLLent
chronograMs IssVeD by I. ʜILton, F.S.A."
= 1885.

More difficult than chronograms are Greek dates, because each letter in Greek has a numerical value, and the numbers do not follow in an uninterrupted series, because certain additional figures are introduced. It is therefore often necessary in cataloguing Greek books to refer to a table such as the following:—

A	α'	1	I	ι'	10	P	ρ'	100
B	β'	2	K	κ'	20	Σ	σ'	200
Γ	γ'	3	Λ	λ'	30	T	τ'	300
Δ	δ'	4	M	μ'	40	Υ	υ'	400
E	ϵ'	5	N	ν'	50	Φ	ϕ'	500
	ς'	6	Ξ	ξ'	60	X	χ'	600
Z	ζ'	7	O	o'	70	Ψ	ψ'	700
H	η'	8	Π	π'	80	Ω	ω'	800
Θ	θ'	9	ϛ	ϟ	90		ϡ	900

It will be noticed that the top letters of each series spell "$\alpha\iota\rho$," which can be borne in mind. The irregularities in the series are final ς' for six, and the invented letters, for 90 and 900. The same series of letters, with the accent beneath instead of above, are used for thousands, as—

$$\acute{\alpha} = 1 \qquad \acute{\iota}\ 10 \qquad \rho' = 100$$
$$\alpha_{\prime} = 1,000 \qquad \iota_{\prime}\ 10,000 \qquad \rho_{\prime} = 100,000$$

There is considerable difficulty in dating books published in France between September 1792, when the French Revolutionary Calendar was introduced, and December 1805, when the Gregorian mode of calculation was restored by Napoleon, because the Revolutionary year began with the autumn. It is impossible therefore, as the months are not usually given in the imprints of books, to tell whether a book dated *an.* 1 was published in 1792 or 1793. It is usual, however, to reckon from 1792, and to count *an.* 8, for instance, as 1800, by which means an approximate date is obtained.

Size-Notation.

When we come to the last piece of description on our catalogue slip, we experience considerable difficulty in certain cases. The statement of the case of size-notation, which has caused so much discussion, and given rise to so many schemes, is so well put by the late Mr. Winter Jones, in his inaugural address at the Conference of Librarians held in London,

October 1877, that I shall transfer it to these pages :—

" One of these points is the designation of the sizes of books. As regards modern books, the folding of the sheets of paper is generally received as the guide, but it is not a guide which speaks to the eye. Some duodecimos may be larger than some octavos, and some octavos may be larger than some folios, to say nothing of the uncertainty of the quartos. When we come to ancient books the matter is still worse. The early printers did not use large sheets of paper and fold them twice or more to form quartos, octavos, etc., but merely folded their paper once, thus making what is now understood by the terms folios or quartos, according to the size of the sheet of paper. Three or more of these sheets were laid one within another, and formed gatherings or quires, each sheet after the first in each gathering being called an inlay.[1] This printing by

[1] It was this practice which confused a correspondent of the *Athenæum*, who published his discovery that the first folio of Shakespeare was not a folio at all.

gatherings was adopted for the convenience of binding. The consequence of this practice would be that the printer would either print one page at a time or two, but no more. If two, he would have to divide the matter to be printed into portions sufficient for eight, twelve, sixteen, or twenty pages, according to the number of inlays in each gathering, and then print, say the first and twelfth, then the second and the eleventh, and so on; and the result of this practice is occasionally seen in an inequality in the length of the pages, particularly in the centre inlay, which would be printed last, and would therefore have either too much or too little matter if the calculation of the quantity necessary for each page had not been exact. It has been suggested that the difficulty might be met by adopting the size of the printed page as the guide, but such a guide would certainly be fallacious. It would not indicate the size of the volume; it would not allow for the many cases of 'oceans of margins and rivers of text;' it would not speak to the eye without opening the book.

The better plan would appear to be to adopt, to a certain extent, the system used by bookbinders. As they regulate their charges according to the size of the millboard required for binding their book, their scale is independent of the folding of the printed sheet. It contains twenty-nine divisions or designations of different sizes, of which twenty-six represent modifications of the five sizes of folio, 4to, 8vo, 12mo, and 18mo, a striking proof of the uncertainty of the sizes supposed to be indicated by these five terms. I speak, of course, of the measure used by English bookbinders. It would certainly be advisable that some rule should be laid down, which might apply to all countries, by which the general sizes of books might be designated, and minute subdivisions be avoided. Why should we designate sizes by paper marks, and talk of pot quartos and foolscap octavos? The pot and the foolscap are things of the past. It would surely be better to adopt some such rule as the following: To designate as 12mo all books not exceeding seven inches in height; as 8vo all those above seven and not exceeding ten inches in height; as 4to those above ten and not exceeding twelve inches in height; and as folio all above twelve inches. The folios might be further described, according to the fact, as *large* or *super*, in order to avoid the various subdivisions of crown, copy, demy medium, royal imperial, elephant, and columbier folio."

At the Exhibition of Library Appliances in connection with the London Conference, Mr. F. Weaklin submitted seven diagrams of eighty-two sizes given to books, from imperial 4to to demy 48mo, and the matter had already been under special consideration in the United States. Mr. Jewett suggested that after the description 8vo, 4to, etc., the exact height and width in inches and tenths of inches should be added between brackets. He measured print; but, as pointed out by Mr. Winter Jones in the above quotation, this measurement overlooks one of the most important points in respect to the character and value of a book, viz., the size of the margin. When the late Sir William Stirling Maxwell wished to adopt Mr.

Jewett's suggestion, I recommended that the width and height of the actual page should be measured, and this was done in *An Essay towards a Collection of Books relating to Proverbs, Emblems, Apophthegms, Epitaphs, and Ana, being a Catalogue of those at Keir* (1860), which I edited for him.

This system of measurement is not needed in a small library, where the ordinary nomenclature is sufficient. The real difficulty underlying the whole subject was pointed out by Mr. Bradshaw in his paper at the Cambridge Meeting of the Library Association, " A Word on Size Notation as distinguished from Form Notation." He there states two facts often overlooked : " (1) That the terms folio, quarto, octavo, etc., represent strictly not size-notation, but form-notation; and (2) That the modern methods of making paper and of printing books combine to render any accurate application of form-notation to such books not so much difficult as impossible. The logical conclusion from these two facts is, of course, that the form-notation expressed by the

terms folio, quarto, octavo, etc., should
be given up in the case of modern books,
to which it is wholly inapplicable; and
that a size-notation which does represent
an undoubted fact, should be adopted in
its place. This logical conclusion was
seen, accepted, and acted upon at Cambridge in the year 1854; and I confess
that it is difficult to resist the conviction
that this principle must sooner or later be
accepted by others, though there will no
doubt be differences of opinion as to the
most advisable form of notation to adopt.
A librarian cannot afford to be eccentric
in this matter; whatever method is adopted,
it must be adopted by all the great libraries,
and it must commend itself to the general
reader. Now I feel sure that I shall not
be taxed with dogmatism or with any
predilection for some crotchet of my own
devising, if I say that the complicated and
artificial systems recommended by the
Committee and others, are such as cannot
possibly become familiar, even if they
become intelligible, to the general run of
readers. In the old Cambridge size-
notation of London 1856, 8 × 5 meaning

eight inches high by five inches across, the second number denoting the breadth very soon fell out of use, except in writing, and for years we always spoke of books as eights, sevens, sixes, etc., meaning that they were eight, seven, or six inches high."

To this passage is added the following note :—

"The practice in use with us has been to measure the height of the book from the top to the bottom of the page, disregarding the cover. We compute inches as we compute a man's age ; a book is eight inches until it is nine inches, only, seeing that bound books are so often cut not quite square, anything short of the number used in the size-notation by the eighth of an inch or less, we call by that number for ordinary purposes. I have said above that in our General Library Catalogue we have reverted to the common form-notation, 8vo, 12mo, etc., but pure size-notation is still retained in other departments, while in Trinity College Library it has never been given up since it was first adopted in 1856 or thereabouts."

The committee referred to by Mr.

Bradshaw was the Size-Notation Committee of the Library Association, of which my brother, the late Mr. B. R. Wheatley, was a member. He took great interest in this subject, and drew up a scale of sizes which might be marked upon an ordinary two-foot rule. He was anxious that " a system should be adopted based on the well-known terms hitherto employed of folio, 4to, 8vo, 12mo, etc., and their qualifying varieties of imperial, royal, etc., with an approximate height and width in inches affixed to each size."

I think that Mr. Bradshaw's argument is convincing against making any arbitrary rule of this kind, and affixing a definite size to every variety of form-designation. But at the same time we must remember that the form-notation has very largely been used for a size-notation, and that bibliographers alone cannot make this change, because publishers, booksellers, and bookbinders all use the notation as well as cataloguers. After all I cannot help thinking that the difficulty has been very greatly exaggerated. Folio and quarto are almost entirely used as terms of form-notation, and they are usually found sufficient except in the case of atlas or elephant folios, which seem to require some distinguishing designation. Nowadays a large number of library books are in what is called demy octavo. This I would distinguish as octavo, and all below that size I would call small octavos, and all above large octavos. Very few modern books are styled duodecimos; therefore that form will not give the cataloguer much trouble. It is clearly useless for the latter to distinguish books by such meaningless terms as foolscap octavo, post octavo, etc., like the publisher. Of course there is the difference in size between old and new books. The ordinary octavo of the old books is a smaller size than the modern octavo, but this will be settled by the date, and among the old books there will be no difficulty in finding duodecimos.

Mr. Nicholson has entered very fully into this question of size-notation in his Bodleian Rules, where he gives two tables as guides for correct description. Rule 57 is: " The size of a book printed on water-marked paper is to be described in accordance with Table I., on unwater-marked paper with Table II."

COLLATION.

In most catalogues the note of the size will finish the entry, but it is a very useful addition when the number of pages of all books in single volumes is given. Sometimes the pages of the book itself only are noted without reference to the preliminary matter, and sometimes the Roman numerals are added on to the Arabic numerals and given as one total; but this latter practice is not to be commended. The best plan is to set down the pages thus—pp. xv, 421 (some put this pp. xv + 421, but the plus sign is not necessary); or if the preliminary matter is not paged, thus—half-title, title, five preliminary leaves, pp. 467.

In the case of very rare and valuable works, a full collation becomes necessary, and such collation should be drawn up according to the plan accepted among bibliographers, which can be seen in the standard bibliographies of early printed books, and such a model bibliography as

Upcott's *Bibliographical Account of the Principal Works relating to English Topography* (3 vols., 8vo, 1818).

Even when it is not thought necessary to give a collation, it will be well to notice if a book contains a portrait, or plates.

CHAPTER V.

 SUPPOSE it may be conceded that in the abstract the most useful kind of catalogue is that which contains the titles and subject references in one alphabet; but in the particular case of a large library this system is not so convenient, because the subject references unnecessarily swell the size of the catalogue, and by their frequency confuse the title entries. For instance, it is something appalling to conjecture what would be the size of the British Museum Catalogue if subject references were included in the general alphabet. In the case of a large library it will be more convenient to have an index of subjects forming a separate alphabet by itself, and this cannot be made until the catalogue of authors is completed. Taking a somewhat arbitrary limit, it may be said

that in libraries containing more than ten
thousand volumes it will be found more
useful to have a distinct index of subjects,
while in catalogues of libraries below that
number it will generally be advisable to
include the subject references with the
titles in one general alphabet.

If all the subject references are reserved
for an index, there will still remain a large
number of references in the general
alphabet which are required for the proper
use of the catalogue ; and here it may be
well to say something as to the nomenclature of references. Mr. Cutter, in the
valuable series of definitions prefixed to
his *Rules for a Dictionary Catalogue*, has
the following :—

" *Reference*, partial registry of a book
(omitting the imprint) under author, title,
subject, or kind, referring to a more full
entry under some other heading ; occasionally used to denote merely entries without
imprints, in which the reference is implied.
The distinction of entry and reference is
almost without meaning for Short, as a
title-a-liner saves nothing by referring
unless there are several references.

"*Analytical reference*, or simply an analytical registry of some part of a book or of some work contained in a collection, referring to the heading under which the book or collection is entered.

"*Cross reference*, reference from one subject to another.

"*Heading reference*, from one form of a heading to another.

"*First-word reference, catch-word reference, subject-word reference*, same as first-word entry, omitting the imprint and referring."

These definitions are important, and it would be well if the distinction here made as to what a cross-reference really is were borne in mind. It has become the practice among bibliographers to describe all references as cross-references. This is the case in the British Museum rules :—

"LV. Cross-references to be divided into three classes, from name to name, from name to work, and from work to work. Those of the first class to contain merely the name, title, or office of the person referred to as entered ; those of the second, so much of the title referred to besides as, together with the size and date, may give the means of at once identifying, under its heading, the book referred to ; those of the third class to contain moreover so much of the title referred from, as may be necessary to ascertain the object of the reference."

The public often cause a still further confusion in words, for they cry out for the shelf-marks to be placed to references. If this be done, they no longer remain references, but become double entries.

There are many disadvantages in this plan of putting press-marks to references, but it is adopted at the British Museum, and it certainly is annoying to have to run from one end of a many-volumed catalogue to another.

In Mr. Nichols's *Handbook for Readers* it is said (p. 42) that "a work is never entered at full length more than once and it is only from the main entry that the book-ticket must be made out." But if the press-marks are added to the references, one would imagine that they are intended to be used, and it is scarcely to be expected that any one will take the trouble to refer to another place when he has sufficient information under his eyes.

Catalogue work is different from index work, where the entries may be duplicated without inconvenience ; but in the case of books, if all the references have press-marks, there is considerable danger of confusion whenever the position of a book is changed. The main entries will be corrected, but some of the references will almost certainly be overlooked. If the books are never moved, there is no great harm in putting press-marks to the references.

It must, I think, be conceded that when the references are so long as they often are in the British Museum Catalogue, and as seems to be contemplated by Mr. Cutter's remark quoted above, they are really duplicate or subsidiary entries rather than references.

There is no real necessity to copy any part of the titles in the great majority of references. Take, for instance, the following two modes of referring from the subject of a biography to the authors :—

Shakespeare :

—— and his Contemporaries.
Nares. 1822. 4to.　27342

—— and his Times.　Drake.
1817.　2 vols.　4to.　7212

—— Biography.　De Quincey.
vol. xv.　8vo.　1808

—— —— Knight.　1842.
8vo.　13296

—— Biographical Memoir.
1825.　8vo.　21294

—— History of.　Fullom.　1864.
8vo.　29492

—— Illustrations of his Life.
Halliwell.　1874.　4to.　47851

—— Life.　Chalmers.　German
trans.　Leipzig.　8vo.　35270

—— —— Halliwell.　1848.
8vo.　10430

—— —— Skottowe.　1824.
2 vols.　8vo.　21673

These entries are taken from a large
heading, and do not come together as they
do here.　By following the wording of
the title in this way you do not get a
true index.　For instance, under this same

main heading of Shakespeare we have in different parts of the sub-alphabet :—

> Illustrated. Lennox.   1753-4.
>   3 vols. 12mo.   13861
> Life. Skottowe. 1824. 2 vols.
>   8vo.   21673
> Plots. Simrock. 1850. 8vo. 21617

All these books are on the plots, and should come together. At present any-one looking at the entry would suppose that there was only one book on the plots of the plays in the library.

Another way of making the references may be set out thus :—

Shakespeare :

> Life : *Chalmers, De Quincey, Fullom* (1864), *Halliwell* (1848), *Knight* (1842), *Skottowe* (1824).
> —— S. and his Contemporaries: *Nares* (1822).
> —— S. and his Times : *Drake* (1817).
> Plots of his Plays : *Lennox* (1753), *Simrock* (1850), *Skottowe* (1824).

Not only does the second plan take up less space, but it is also the more convenient, as giving the required information in the clearest manner.

All references should be in English,[1] and the subject of the book should be used for the reference rather than the often periphrastic form of the title. Thus, in making a subject reference for the following book :—

> Mudie (Robert). The Feathered Tribes of the British Islands. 1834. 2 vols.

—the reference must be from "Birds" or "Ornithology," as it will be useless to refer from "Feathered Tribes."

No reference should be made to a title which does not indicate the information sought for. Thus, if a work contains an account of some subject which is not specified on the title, this must not be referred to unless a note is added to the title to show that the book does contain this information. Sometimes one reference will be sufficient for a group of titles. Thus, in referring from one form of an author's name to another, it is not necessary to

[1] Always use the word *see* in preference to *vide.*

repeat the titles under that author's name even in the shortest manner.

It is not well in subject references included in an alphabetical catalogue or in an alphabetical index of subjects to classify at all. Thus *Gold* should be under *G*, and *Silver* under *S*; and at the end of the heading of Metals or Metallurgy such cross-references as these can be added : "See also *Gold, Silver.*"

It is not easy to calculate the average number of references to a given number of chief entries. If we exclude subject references, it may be roughly put at about a third. If subject references are included, it will be about two to one, or twice as many references as titles. Many titles will only require one reference, but others will help to turn the balance,—as, for instance, the following, which will require ten references :—

The Life of Haydn, in a Series of Letters written at Vienna [originally written in Italian by G. Carpani], followed by the Life of Mozart [by A. H. F. von Slichtegroll], with

Observations on Metastasio, and on
the Present State of Music in France
and Italy. Translated from the
French of L. A. C. Bombet, with
Notes by the Author of the Sacred
Melodies [W. Gardiner]. London,
1817. 8vo.

In the first place, Bombet is a pseudonym
for Henri Beyle; therefore, according to
the rule adopted in· the catalogue, there
must be a different reference. If the
title is placed under Beyle, then there
must be a reference from Bombet; and if
under the pseudonym, there must be a
reference from Beyle. There must be
references from Haydn, Mozart, and
Metastasio, from Slichtegroll, Carpani,
and Gardiner, from Music, and possibly
from France and Italy.

The specimen page here given will
show how a subject index may be incorporated in one alphabet with an
author's catalogue :—

Case.	Shelf.		Size.	Date.
II	2	SHUTTLEWORTH (Philip N.). The Consistency of the whole scheme of Revelation with itself and with Human Reason.		
LL	3	London. — Paraphrastic Translation of the Apostolical Epistles, with Notes.	12°	1832
		London.	8°	1840
		SIBERIA		
		Travels : *Dobell* (1830)		
		SICILY		
		Travels, etc.: *Brydone* (1790), *Hoare* (1819), *Swinburne* (1783), *Smyth* (1824)		
		— Volcanoes of : *Hamilton* (1772)		
		— Vestiges of Antient Manners : *Blunt* (1823)		
		SIDMOUTH (Viscount) Life : *Pellew* (1847)		

It will be noticed that in the case of references the word *see* is omitted. If the names to be referred to, which follow a colon, are printed in italic, or, in the case of a manuscript catalogue, are under-scored with red ink, they will be clearly distinguishable without the word *see*, and a wearisome repetition will be avoided. In the case of cross-references at the end to some other heading [see also], it will be more convenient to use the word than to omit it.

Panizzi was an advocate for a Subject Index, or " Index of Matters," as he called it,[1] but he did not venture to recommend such a work officially to the trustees.[2] He was fully examined on this subject before the Commission in 1849, and he referred to a memorandum which he had submitted to the Council of the Royal Society when employed upon their catalogue. He there writes :—

" A catalogue of a library is intended

[1] This expression is often used, although it can scarcely be considered as English.
[2] See his answer to question 9892, *Minutes of Evidence, Commission* 1849.

principally to give an accurate inventory
of the books which it comprises; and is
in general consulted either to ascertain
whether a particular book is in the collection, or to find what works it contains on
a given subject. To obtain these ends,
classed catalogues have been compiled,
in which the works are systematically
arranged according to their subjects.
Many distinguished individuals in different
countries have drawn up catalogues of
this description, but no two of them have
agreed on the same plan of classification;
and even those who have confessedly
followed the system of another person
have fancied it necessary to depart in
some particulars from their model. . . .
Those who want either to consult a book,
of which they only know the subject, or
to find what books on a particular subject
are in the library, can obtain this information (as far as it can be collected from a
title-page, which is all that can be expected in a catalogue) more easily from
an index of matters to an alphabetical
catalogue than by any other means. Here
also nothing is left to discretion as far

as concerns order. Entries, being short cross-references, are in a great measure avoided ; and repetitions, far from being inconvenient, will save the time and trouble of looking in more places than one in order to find what is wanted. . . . The plan which is proposed was adopted by Dr. Watt in his *Bibliotheca Britannica,* the usefulness of which work must be acknowledged by every one conversant with bibliography. That it would not be so useful had any systematical arrangement been followed seems undeniable. The vast plan of the *Bibliotheca Britannica,* however, did not allow its author to give, either to the titles of the books or to the index, that extent which ought to be given to both in the Catalogue of the Library of the Royal Society" (*Minutes of Evidence,* p. 704).

Although here Panizzi makes the sound remark that the information to be expected in a catalogue is that which is found in the title-page, he had previously expressed a considerably more comprehensive opinion. He wrote :—

"The catalogue of a library like that

13

of the Royal Society should be as complete as possible; that is, it should give
all the information requisite concerning
any book which may be the object of
inquiry. Whether a work be printed
separately, or in a collection—whether it
extend to the greater part of a folio
volume, or occupy only part of a single
leaf—no distinction should be made; the
title of each should be separately entered.
Hence every one of the *Memoirs* or
papers in the acts of academies; every
one of the articles in scientific journals or
collections, whatever they may be, should
have its separate place in the catalogue.
Thus, for instance, all the letters in
Hanschius' Collection should be entered
in their proper places under the writers'
names. It is only by carrying this principle to the FULLEST extent that a catalogue can be called COMPLETE, and a
library, more particularly of books relating
to science, made as useful as it is capable
of being. This, however, would make a
great difference in the expense, and take
considerable time."

A little consideration will show that

such an extensive principle of action could not be practically carried out, and we may well ask whether it would be advisable to adopt such a plan even if it could be carried out. We regret the waste of labour spent in cataloguing the same book over and over again, but how much greater would be the waste of labour and money if the managers of every library which contained the *Philosophical Magazine* thought it necessary to include the whole contents of that periodical in its catalogue ! The labour of cataloguing these series is the work of bibliographers, and such valuable books of reference as the *Royal Society Catalogue of Scientific Papers* and Poole's *Index of Periodical Literature* are suitable for all libraries.

To return to the mode of carrying out a subject index, it may be again remarked that it is not necessary to follow the titles textually, and if the titles are so followed there can be no advantage in making the references longer than in Watt's *Bibliotheca*. In primary entries the titles must be accurately followed, but in references it is often much more convenient to dispense with the wording chosen by the author. Two books with totally different titles are often identical in subject, and the indexer saves the time of the consulter by realizing this fact and acting upon it.

I think that any one who compares the system adopted in the indexes to the Catalogues of the Library of the Athenæum Club and of the London Library with that of, say, the Catalogue of the Manchester Free Library, 1881, will at once see how much more readily the former can be used.

Mr. Parry, in his answer 7351 (*Minutes*, p. 470), advocates the plan of having a separate index of subjects, and in spite of all that has been said in favour of dictionary catalogues, I hold that this is the simplest and most useful for students; although for popular libraries there is much to be said in favour of dictionary catalogues. One of the most elaborate indexes I know is that by my brother, Mr. B. R. Wheatley, for the Catalogue of the Royal Medical and Chirurgical Society. By this plan he who knows what he wants finds it without being confused by, to him, useless references, while he who does not know can consult the index.

In an index the headings will of course be in alphabet, and the sub-headings may be so also; but often some system of classification will be better. No hard-and-fast rule can be made for all cases. But it is usually better to bring the subjects of the books together, regardless of the wording of the title.

CHAPTER VI.

ARRANGEMENT.

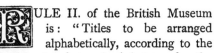ULE II. of the British Museum is: "Titles to be arranged alphabetically, according to the English alphabet only (whatever be the order of the alphabet in which a foreign name might have been entered in its original language);" and this rule has been generally followed. Mr. Cutter (rule 169) adds to this, "Treat I and J, U and V, as separate letters;" and every consulter of the British Museum Catalogue must wish that this rule was adopted there, for anything so confusing as this unnecessary mixing of the letters I and J and U and V it is scarcely possible to imagine. Mr. Cutter goes on: "ij, at least in the olden Dutch names, should be arranged as y; do not put Spanish names beginning with Ch, Ll, Ñ, after all other names

beginning with C, L, and N, as is done by the Spanish Academy."

The Museum rule (XIII.) is : "German names in which the letters ä, ö, or ü occur, to be spelt with the diphthong æ, œ, and ue respectively."

Mr. Cutter follows this, and adds to it (rule 25) :—

"In Danish names, if the type å is not to be had, use its older equivalent *aa;* in a manuscript catalogue the modern orthography ä should be employed. Whatever is chosen should be uniformly used, however the names may appear in the books. The diphthong æ should not be written ae, nor should ö be written oe; ö, not œ, should be used for ø.

"In Hungarian names write ö, ü, with the diæresis (not oe, ue), and arrange like the English o, u.

"The Swedish names, ä, å, ö, should be so written (not ae, oe), and arranged as the English a, o."

The Cambridge rule (10) is as follows : "German and Scandinavian names, in which the forms ä, ö, ü, å, occur, to be treated, for the purpose of alphabetical sequence, as if spelt with ae, oe, and ao respectively. In German names ä, ö, ü, to be printed ae, oe, ue."

The Library Association rule (44) is: "The German ä, ö, ü, are to be arranged as if written out in full ae, oe, ue."

The first part of the Cambridge rule and the whole of that of the Library Association is likely to lead to confusion. The only safe way to deal with these letters is either to spell them out, or to arrange them as if they were English letters. The English alphabet must be pre-eminent in an English catalogue.

The rule that M', Mc, St., etc., should be arranged as if spelt Mac, Saint, etc., stands on a different basis from the above, and the reason is, as stated by Mr. Cutter (rule 173), "because they are so pronounced." When we see St., we at once say Saint, and therefore look under Sa.

The Index Society rule enters fully into this point, and explains what is a difficulty to some: "6. Proper names with the prefix St., as St. Albans, St. John, to be arranged in the alphabet as if written in

full, *Saint*. When the word *Saint* represents a ceremonial title, as in the case of
St. Alban, St. Giles, and St. Augustine,
these names to be arranged under the
letters A and G respectively; but the
places St. Albans, St. Giles, and St.
Augustine will be found under the prefix
Saint. The prefixes M' and Mc to be
arranged as if written in full, Mac."

When several titles follow one heading,
it is necessary to use a dash in place of
repeating the heading, and there are one
or two points worthy of attention in
respect to this dash.

The Library Association rule is: " 35.
The heading is not to be repeated; a single
indent or dash indicates the omission of
the preceding heading or title."

The Index Society rule is rather fuller :
" 17. A dash, instead of an indentation,
to be used as a mark of repetition. The
dash to be kept for entries exactly similar,
and the word to be repeated when the
second differs in any way from the first.
The proper name to be repeated when
that of a different person. In the case
of joint authors the Christian names or

initials of the first, whose surname is arranged in the alphabet, to be in parentheses, but the Christian names of the second to be in the natural order, as *Smith* (John) and Alexander *Brown*, not *Smith* (John) and *Brown* (Alexander)."

The reason for the last direction is that the Christian name is only brought back in order to make the alphabetical position of the surname clear; and as this is not necessary in respect to the second person, the names should remain in their natural order.

Dashes should be of a uniform length, and that length should not be too great. It is a great mistake to suppose that the dash is to be the length of the line which is not repeated. If it is necessary to mark the repetition of a portion of the title as well as the author, this should be indicated by another dash, and not by the elongation of the former one; thus :—

Milton (John), Works in Verse and Prose,
    Printed from the Original Editions,
    with Life by the Rev. John Mitford.
    8 vols. 8vo. London, 1851.

Milton (*continued*).

—— Poetical Works, with Notes, Life, etc., by the Rev. H. J. Todd. 6 vols. 8vo. London, 1801.

—— —— —— Second Edition. 7 vols. royal 8vo. London, 1809.

—— —— with Notes, edited by Sir Egerton Brydges. 6 vols. small 8vo. London, 1853.

All the dashes except the first, which represents the author's name, can be got rid of by using the words [the same] or [another edition], etc.

In the alphabetization of a catalogue the prefixes in personal names, even when printed separately, are to be treated as if they were joined ; thus :—

De Montfort.	De Quincey.
Demophilus.	Des Barres.
De Morgan.	Du Chaillu.
Demosthenes.	

In the case of compound words a different plan, however, is to be adopted. Each word is to be treated as separate, and arranged accordingly. The Index

Society rule is as follows : " 4. Headings consisting of two or more distinct words are not to be treated as integral portions of one word ; thus the arrangement should be :—

Grave, John		Grave at Kherson
Grave at Kherson		Grave, John
Grave of Hope	not	Gravelot
Grave Thoughts		Grave of Hope
Gravelot		Gravesend
Gravesend		Grave Thoughts

Mr. Cutter enters very fully into this point of arrangement in his rules.

It is a very frequent mistake to over-look the fact that the Christian name placed after a surname is merely there for the sake of convenience, and to make it take its place with the words that follow in their natural position. For instance, in the above examples John Grave stands at the head, because Grave is the only portion that can be considered in the alphabet. If, however, there was a Charles or a Henry Grave, they would take their position above John Grave, because their Christian names are all in the same category.

The order in which the entries under an author's name should be arranged is dealt with in the British Museum rules LXIX. to LXXVII., but it is not necessary to quote all these in this place.

The Library Association rules put the matter very succinctly :—

" 38. The works of an author are to be arranged in the following order :—

" *a*. Collected works.

" *b*. Partial collections.

" *c*. Individual works in alphabetical order of titles, under the first word not an article or a preposition having the meaning of ' concerning.'

" Translations are to follow the originals in alphabetical order of languages."

The Cambridge Rule is as follows :—

" 38. The works of an author to be entered in the following order :—

" (1) Collected works in the original language.

" (2) Translations of collected works.

" (3) Collections of two or more works.

" (4) Separate works.

" (5) Entire portions of a separate work to follow that work.

" (6) Selections or collected fragments."

This question of arrangement is distinctly one which may be modified according to the special needs of a particular library. It only becomes a question of importance in a very large library, because in a small library the number of entries under one author are not often very numerous. I should take exception to the arrangement of separate works in alphabetical order, because in the case of titles other than those of plays, poems, novels, etc. (which have arbitrary titles), there is little that is suitable for such arrangement, and it is practically no order at all. I should prefer the chronological order as the most useful for reference. In the case of those authors whose works are voluminous, some system of classification of the separate works is needed. Thus Milton's prose works should be arranged separately from his poems.

It is also a question whether translations should not be kept together at the end. Abstracts of the contents of collected editions of an author's works greatly add to the convenience of a catalogue. It is almost a necessity in a lending library, as by this means you can send for the particular volume you require. The adoption of the plan at the British Museum would save a reader from sending for a whole set of books when he only wants one volume. Mr. Parry, in his evidence before the Commission, alludes to this point. He said: "I remember there was one rule as to collected works, that each separate work in the collection was to be expressed upon the title that we wrote, and afterwards printed separately under the collected heading in the catalogue; that was abandoned, I remember, and I certainly thought it was an important abandonment: it was the abandonment, as it seemed to me, of a useful principle; but it was abandoned, I believe, for the purpose of expediting the catalogue; and in all respects we endeavoured as much as possible to shorten our labour consistently with accuracy" (p. 467).

Mr. Cutter deals with this point in his

rule 197 : "Arrange *contents* either in
the order of the volumes or alphabetically by the titles of the articles." After
giving an example, he adds : "It is evi-
dent how much more compendious the
second method is. But there is no reason
why an alphabetical 'contents' should not
be run into a single paragraph.

"The titles of novels and plays contained in any collection ought to be
entered in the main alphabet; it is
difficult then to see the advantage of an
alphabetical arrangement of the same
titles under the collection. Many other
collections are composed of works for
which alphabetical order is no gain,
because the words of their titles are not
mnemonic words, and it is not worth
while to take the trouble of arranging
them; but there are others composed of
both classes in which such order may be
convenient."

We have been considering the arrangement of the titles of ordinary books, but
here it will be necessary to go back
somewhat, and ask what we have to
catalogue. We may have printed books,

newspapers, manuscripts (including auto-
graphs), prints and drawings, and maps.
Newspapers may be included with printed
books, but the rest must, without doubt,
be kept distinct. When these different
classes are small, they can with advantage
be catalogued separately at the end of the
general catalogue ; but when any or all of
them are large, they must be treated as distinct subjects, and catalogued according to
special rules which cannot be given here.

What is a printed book? Some have
made a distinction between tracts (or
pamphlets) and books ; but any definition
of the former, intended to distinguish
them from the latter, which has been
attempted has always failed to satisfy
the bibliographer. It is only necessary
to imagine the confusion that would be
caused in the library of the British
Museum if the titles were thus sorted
to see the futility of any such distinction.
The only excuse for a separate catalogue
of pamphlets is in the case of those
libraries which possess a large number
of ephemeral pamphlets, bound up in a
long series, and kept distinct. Here, as

14

the pamphlets are only occasionally required, it may be found unadvisable to
fill the general catalogue with uninterest-
ing entries. It may be supposed that the
last remark, as recognizing the existence
of a pamphlet, is contradictory to that
which goes before, but it is not really so.
There is no doubt of the existence of a
something which is undoubtedly a pamphlet, but there is no rule by which some
other small book can be distinguished as
a pamphlet or not. The special characteristic of a pamphlet does not entirely
consist in the number of pages, for books
in which the most momentous discoveries
have been announced have been made
up of few leaves, and it does not entirely
consist in the importance or otherwise of
the subject.

There is one class of pamphlets which
gives the cataloguer much trouble, viz.,
Extracts from Journals and Transactions.
If these are catalogued without any indication that they are excerpts, readers of
the catalogue are misled into the belief
in the existence of separate books which
were never issued. At the same time

the catalogue is unnecessarily enlarged if the full particulars as to the title of the journal from which the pamphlet has been extracted are given. If there are many of these titles it will be well to adopt some sign, such as a dagger, at the beginning of the title to indicate the character of the pamphlet.

When we have decided to arrange in one general alphabet the titles of ordinary books, both those whose authors are known and those which are anonymous, we are still left with a large number of books which are different in character from ordinary books. We then have to decide how to deal with journals and transactions, ephemerides, observations, reports, etc. These classes of works are generally kept distinct, but are included in the general alphabet as academies or transactions, periodical publications or journals. In the case of comparatively small private libraries, there is no need for the separation at all, as these seldom contain many journals or transactions; but if it be advisable to make the distinction, I think the balance of advantage

is on the side of keeping the class outside
the alphabet, chiefly for the reason that
inner alphabets are confusing and dis-
advantageous.

There are two main reasons in favour
of the separation of serials, periodicals,
or whatever other name we may give
the class. The theoretical reason is,
that they are not like other books, and
that the rules for one will not apply to
the other. It is agreed, on all hands,
that MSS. should be separated from
printed books, and yet a MS. is often
more like a printed book than a journal
is like a distinct treatise. I mean that
in the one case the difference is merely
one of production,—print or writing,—and
in the other it is a structural difference
of the mode of composition.

The practical reason is, that you elimi-
nate the chief disturbing elements of a
catalogue. The catalogue of ordinary
books, if well made in the first instance,
requires little alteration, and needs only
additions ; but the catalogue of serials,
by the very nature of its contents, wants
continued change.

Some librarians who have followed the British Museum rules continue the terms adopted there of *Academies* and *Periodical Publications ;* but I think the headings *Transactions* and *Journals* are in every way preferable. The word *Academy* is entirely foreign to our habits, and most of those academies which exist here are institutions quite distinct from societies which publish transactions. Almost the only exception to this rule is the Royal Irish Academy. Even abroad, societies are more numerous than academies.[1] With respect to the heading *Periodical Publications*, it may be said that transactions would logically come as properly under it as journals and magazines, because all are published periodically.

This subject of the arrangement of periodicals has not been treated of so exhaustively as it deserves. Mr. J. B. Bailey communicated a paper on "Some Points to be Considered in Preparing Catalogues of Transactions and Periodicals" to the Library Association of the

[1] Was it not Christopher North's Shepherd who said, "Open a school and call it an academy"?

United Kingdom in February 1880,[1] in which he affirms that so little agreement is there among cataloguers, that the three most recent catalogues of scientific transactions and periodicals then published were arranged on different plans. The three catalogues referred to were (1) *Catalogue of Scientific Serials*, 1633—1876, by S. H. Scudder, Cambridge, U.S., 1879; (2) *Catalogue of the Library of the Royal Medical and Chirurgical Society*, London, 1879; (3) *Catalogue of the Library of the Museum of Practical Geology and Geological Survey*, London, 1878.

At the Cambridge Meeting of the Library Association, 1882, I communicated a paper entitled " Thoughts on the Cataloguing of Journals and Transactions." In this paper I discussed some of the open questions respecting their arrangement, and these points I may recapitulate here. Mr. Bailey is in favour of Mr. Scudder's union of journals and transactions in one catalogue, but he is not so satisfied that the plan of arranging

[1] *Monthly Notices*, No. 2.

these under the names of the places of publication adopted by that bibliographer is the best.

The two chief questions which arise, after we have settled the point that these serials shall be kept distinct from the general alphabet, are these :—

(1) Shall journals and transactions be treated as one and the same class, or shall they be arranged in separate alphabets ?

(2) If journals and transactions are kept distinct, how shall they be arranged ?

I.

Mr. Scudder, as already mentioned, treats journals and transactions as one and the same class, and arranges both together, according to a combined geographical and alphabetical system. This is, I think, an inconvenient arrangement for a catalogue, for the following reason : Transactions are nearly always known by the names of the places where they are issued, but journals are not known by the name of the place of publication.

For instance, suppose a reader comes to the librarian for the *Jahrbuch* of the *Physikalischer Verein,* the librarian would naturally ask, Which one of these societies? and the reader might answer Frankfort ; but if the *Canadian Journal* were required it is probable that neither reader nor librarian would remember whether it were published at Toronto or at Montreal. The society of its very nature has a local habitation, while the journal has a name, but is not necessarily associated with the place where it is published. It therefore follows that if the titles of the two kinds of periodicals are arranged on different systems, it will be better to keep them distinct than to unite them in one alphabet. In the British Museum Catalogue the two classes are kept distinct, but both are arranged under the names of places, so that they might quite as well have been united in one alphabet. The reason for separation entirely depends, it seems to me, upon the difference of arrangement adopted for each.

II.

Mr. Cutter's rules on this question of arrangement may be considered best under the respective headings of Transactions and Journals.

Transactions.

Mr. Cutter says (rule 40) :—

" Societies are authors of their journals, memoirs, proceedings, transactions, publications. . . . The chief practices in regard to societies have been to enter them (1. British Museum) under a special heading —*Academies*—with a geographical arrangement ; (2. Boston Public Library, printed catalogue) under the name of the place where they have their headquarters ; (3. Harvard College Library and Boston Public Library, present system) under the name of the place, if it enters into the legal name of the society, otherwise under the first word of that name not an article ; (4. Boston Athenæum) English societies under the first word of the society's name not an article ; foreign societies under the name of the place. Both 3. and 4. put under the place all purely local societies, those

whose membership or objects are confined to the place. The first does not
deserve a moment's consideration; such
a heading is out of place in an author-
catalogue, and the geographical arrangement only serves to complicate matters,
and render it more difficult to find any
particular academy. The second is utterly
unsuited to American and English societies.
The third practice is simple; but it is
difficult to see the advantage of the exception which it makes to its general rule of
entry under the society's name; the exception does not help the cataloguer, for
it is just as hard to determine whether
the place enters into the *legal* name as to
ascertain the name; it does not help the
reader, for he has no means of knowing
whether the place is part of the legal name
or not. The fourth is simple and intelligible; it is usually easy for both cataloguer
and reader to determine whether a society
is English or foreign. . . .

"Fifth Plan, Rule 1. Enter academies,
associations, institutes, universities, libraries, galleries, museums, colleges, and all
similar bodies, both English and foreign,

according to their corporate name, neglecting an initial article when there is one.

"*Exception* 1. Enter the royal academies of Berlin, Göttingen, Leipzig, Lisbon, Madrid, Munich, St. Petersburg, Vienna, etc., and the 'Institut' of Paris under those cities. An exception is an evil; this one is adopted because the academies are usually known by the name of the cities, and are hardly ever referred to by the name Königliches, Real, etc."

I cannot agree with Mr. Cutter's remarks in the above extracts. After a pretty extensive experience of the cataloguing of transactions, I have found plan No. 2 far and away the most convenient for reference; it has its own peculiar difficulties, but these are really much fewer than in any of the other plans, and I entirely fail to see why it should be stigmatized as "utterly unsuited to American and English societies." No doubt a large number of societies come under the heading of London, but most large towns in the country have their societies, and the societies of Dublin, Edinburgh, Glasgow,

Liverpool, and Manchester all find their proper places in the alphabet.

The fourth plan may be simple, but it is far from logical, and some good reason is required for the adoption of separate rules for English and foreign societies.

Exception 1 is surely unnecessary, for the publications of the Société Météorologique de France have just as much right to appear under " Paris " as the publications of the " Institut " (which, by the way, is the " Institut " of France, not of Paris).

The difficulties of this first word (not an article) arrangement are numerous. For instance, all the French societies will be under *Société*, and a large number of the English societies under *Royal.* Then, again, how many German and Swiss towns have a *Naturforschende Gesellschaft* —the confusion of which is obviated by arranging them under the names of the towns. This is one reason; but another is, that many of these societies have double titles, with the designation of the society in different languages. For instance, the *Neue Deukschiften* of the " Allgemeine

Schweizerische Gesellschaft für die gesa-
murten Naturwissenschaften," at Zürich,
is also styled *Nouveaux Mémoires de la
Société Helvétique des Sciences Naturelles ;*
and this at once confuses the society with
"Schweizerische Naturforschende Gesellschaft," which is also named "Allgemeine
Schweizerische Gesellschaft " and "Société
Helvétique des Sciences Naturelles."
Several of the Scandinavian societies have
a Latin as well as a native name. Thus the
"Kongl. Vetenskaps Societet," of Upsala,
is also called " Regia Societas Scientiarum
Upsaliensis," and its publications are
known as *Acta* and *Nota Acta.* Again,
the publications of the " Kongelige Norske
Videnskabers Selskab," of Trondhjem,
have been in German as well as in Danish,
and in the former language the style of
the society has taken the two forms
of "Drontheimische Gesellschaft" and
of "Konigl. Norwegische Gesellschaft."
Again, Bohemian societies have both a
German and a Bohemian title, and the
cataloguer must choose which he will take.

It cannot be said that by arranging the
societies under the names of the places

where they meet all difficulties are over-come, but it may safely be said that they are found with much greater ease by the consulter of the catalogue, than if they were spread about in the alphabet under the first words of their titles (not an article), and this, I think, is the greatest advantage that can be claimed for any cataloguing scheme. Another good reason for placing the societies under their place of meeting is that their transactions are most commonly referred to as the " Paris Mémoires," the " Berlin Abhandlungen," or the "Copenhagen Skrifter;" and therefore it is most objectionable that the reader who knows what he wants should have, before consulting the catalogue, to seek for the exact wording of the society's name.

The London Mathematical Society would come under *London* by Cutter's rule, although it is always spoken of as the Mathematical Society simply ; while some of the publications of the Meteorological Society would be arranged under B (British Meteorological Society) and others under M (Meteorological Society). Those who have little to do with transactions can scarcely guess the confusion that occurs in catalogues when the references are not arranged upon a sound system.

There are two very serious objections to the geographical arrangement of the places where societies are seated rather than the alphabetical. One is, that you have to think what country the place is in before looking for it; and the other, that the boundaries of Europe are constantly being altered. If every society is placed under the name of the town where it holds its meetings, and the towns are arranged in one general alphabet, we have an arrangement that is simplicity itself.

It is of paramount importance to place all the publications of a society under one heading, even when the place of meeting may have been changed; and in such a case as this the only safe plan is to arrange all under the name of the last place of meeting, with cross-references from the other places. A good instance of this is the well-known set of transactions which is almost invariably quoted as the *Nova Acta*. The " Kaiserliche Leopoldino-Carolinische Deutsche Akademie der Naturforscher" published their *Acta* at Nuremberg between 1730 and 1754, and their *Nova Acta* at the same place between 1757 and 1791. The *Nova Acta* has subsequently been published at Erlangen, Breslau, and Bonn, and the present seat of the academy is at Dresden.

There is of course a difficulty in the case of peripatetic societies both national (such as the British Association) and international (such as the Congress of Prehistoric Archæology); but these societies have usually permanent headquarters, and these may be treated as the headings.

No mention has been made of what we rather vaguely style " Publishing Societies," because these require special rules. They should be catalogued with a general entry under the division of Transactions, but the separate books published by each society must be catalogued in the general catalogue.

Journals.

Mr. Cutter's rule, No. 54 (*Rules for a Dictionary Catalogue*, p. 53), is as follows: " Periodicals are to be treated as anonymous, and entered under the first word. Ex. *Popular* Science Monthly, *Littell's* Living Age.

" When a periodical changes its title, the whole may be catalogued under the original title, with an explanatory note there, and a reference from the new title to the old ; or each part may be catalogued under its own title, with references : ' For a continuation *see* ;' ' For ten previous volumes *see* .'

"Make a reference from the name of the editor when the periodical is commonly called by his name, as is the case with Silliman's *Journal of Science. . . .*"

I agree, generally, with this rule, but I think that we must arrange somehow that the whole of a journal should appear in one place in the catalogue, however much the title may have been changed. Thus the title of the well-known *Philosophical Magazine* has undergone many changes, but all should appear under the heading of "*Philosophical Magazine.*" The first series is known as *Tilloch's Philosophical Magazine,* and the current series as the

15

*London, Edinburgh, and Dublin Philo-
sophical ·Magazine and Journal.*

Although the rule should be to place
the titles under the first word not an
article, some judgment must be displayed.
Thus the *New Monthly Magazine* should
be placed under " New," because it was
a rival and not a continuation of the
Monthly Magazine ; but the *Neue Notizen*
of Froriep must come under " Notizen,"
of which it is a second series.

As a rule, it is objectionable to place
journals under their editors' names, because editors are continually changing.
For instance, the famous German scientific
journal (*Annalen der Physik*) which was
for so many years associated with the
name of Poggendorff no longer bears the
name of that distinguished man. After
his death his name entirely disappeared
from the title-page.

Something must also be said respecting
astronomical and meteorological observations, reports of various institutions,
surveys, etc. These are not strictly
transactions ; but the same principle which
makes it expedient to take transactions

out of the general alphabet applies to these books. Observations are sometimes catalogued under the name of the observer; but this is a bad practice, because the observer changes, and it is only the observatory which is permanent, and this should be arranged under the place where the observatory is situated, as Greenwich, Paris, etc. The treatment of reports is a more difficult matter, and here again judgment must be called into play. A particular report on a special subject must be treated as a book; but the series of reports of commissions, or the annual reports of an institution as serials, may well be brought under a separate division.

CHAPTER VII.

SOMETHING ABOUT MSS.

ERY little need be said here about the cataloguing of manuscripts, because it is a distinct art from the cataloguing of printed books; but most libraries contain a few manuscripts, and therefore it is needful to say something.

What a large collection of .MSS. really is, is partly answered by Mr. Maunde Thompson, late Keeper of the MSS., and now Principal Librarian, British Museum, in an interesting paper, "On the Arrangement and Preservation of Manuscripts," read before the Library Association in 1886. Mr. Thompson writes:—

"While in foreign countries it is the custom to subdivide and deposit in different custodies the several classes of MSS. after their kind, in England the Museum is the only national institution where MSS. of all descriptions are purchased for the public use. In the Department of MSS., accordingly, may be found every kind of MS., from papyri dating back to the second century before Christ down to the correspondence of our own day on which the ink is scarcely dry. Papyri, ancient and mediæval MSS. of all periods and in all languages from the fifth to the fifteenth century and later, illuminated MSS., literary works of all periods, state papers and literary and private correspondence, charters and rolls, seals, casts of seals, and bullæ—all these are brought together under the custody of the keepers."[1]

Now very few of these rare objects will be found in ordinary libraries. The manuscripts to be found there will probably be literary works, historical and literary correspondence, and perhaps some deeds or family documents. If the manuscripts consist only of a few unprinted literary works or original manuscripts afterwards printed, these may well be included in the general catalogue of printed books. When

[1] *Library Chronicle,* vol. iv., pp. 33-9.

there are autograph letters and miscellaneous MSS., these must be kept separate.
The cataloguer must then consult the best
catalogues of collections of manuscripts,
and choose the plan best suited to his
particular purpose. A collection of autograph letters will best be catalogued under
the names of the writers, arranged in alphabetical order; while a series of historical
documents will often be more conveniently
arranged in chronological order.

The usual mode of cataloguing adopted
is to register the contents of the particular
collection of manuscripts in the order
which it stands, and then to make a full
index. The result of this plan is the
production of a series of volumes of great
interest to the reader. Many a pleasant
and instructive hour may be spent in the
turning over of the pages of such catalogues as that of the Harleian Collection,
or of the various volumes which contain
the descriptions of the additional manuscripts in the British Museum.

There is, however, a great want of a
general catalogue or general index to the
vast collections of the British Museum.

The production of such a work would cause so large an expenditure of labour that perhaps we can scarcely expect it to be produced; but I venture to think that something might be done to bring the very miscellaneous collection of catalogues into some more uniform system than it is at present. The subject index which can be referred to in the MS. room is a work of the greatest value, and he who turns over a few pages of a few of the volumes of which this subject catalogue consists will obtain a more vivid idea o the exceeding richness of the MS. Department of the British Museum than by any other means. This classified catalogue we owe to Mr. Bond, formerly Keeper of the MSS., and late Principal Librarian, and every scholar must feel deep gratitude to him for this great gift of knowledge. If this were printed, it would form a work of immense value; but probably before this could be done it would be necessary to re-catalogue on one system a large number of the entries.

With the present catalogues at the Reading Room table, when a certain

known manuscript is required, the searcher
goes at once to the special catalogue, and
he has little or no difficulty. If he wants
to find a manuscript upon a particular
subject, he can look at the subject catalogue ; but if he wants to find all the
manuscripts of a given book, he will have
to look up the separate indexes of the
different collections. This will be a long
and tedious undertaking, and the searcher
will usually need the assistance of the
gentlemen of the Department—assistance
which is always freely and courteously
rendered.

Catalogues of certain classes of manuscripts have been produced which are of
monumental value; but I think a great
desideratum is a catalogue of all the
distinct works in the Manuscript Department, with information respecting the
printing of such as have been printed.
Possibly such a work, by which can be
found the MS. copies of the works of our
great authors,—and, for the matter of that,
of our small ones too,—is being prepared.
It will be a work of great labour, and if
the Department prepare it, the learning of

the country will be placed under a lasting
obligation.

We may look forward to a time when
a national bibliography of our literature
shall be produced, in which manuscripts
will be registered as well as printed books.
One great characteristic of manuscripts is
the permanence of their reference numbers.
Printed books are moved and change
their shelf-marks, but the number of a
manuscript is always the same.   Sometimes the manuscript is known by the name
of the collection with its number, and
sometimes the reference is to a former
shelf-mark; but if originally a shelf-mark,
it is continued as a part of the manuscript,
however much the original position in the
library may have been changed.

Catalogues of manuscripts are more distinctly literary works than are catalogues
of printed books. Thus Mr. G. F. Warner's
*Catalogue of the Manuscripts and Muni-
ments of Alleyn's College of God's Gift at
Dulwich* (1881) forms an indispensable
portion of any Shakespearian or dramatic
library. The various catalogues of manuscripts in the Bodleian Library, and the

Catalogue of the Cambridge University Manuscripts,[1] are additions to general literature of a very high character.

[1] *Catalogue of the Manuscripts Preserved in the Library of the University of Cambridge.* Edited for the Syndics of the University Press, vol. i., 1856; vol. ii., 1857; vol. iii., 1858; vol. iv., 1861 ; vol. v., 1867. *Index* by H. R. Luard, 1867. 8vo.

CHAPTER VIII.

HEADINGS.

UTHOR.—1. All books to be entered under their authors' surnames; when there are two or more authors, the first is to be taken as the leading name. [75]

2. Foreign compound names to be arranged under the first name. English compound names under the last, except in those cases where the first is known to be a true surname. [76]

3. Proper names of foreigners to be alphabetically arranged under the prefixes Dal, Del, Della, Des, Du, Le, La; but not under the prefixes D', Da, De, Von, Van, Van der. English names to

[1] The number at the end of each rule refers to the page of this book where the reason for the particular rule is more fully discussed.

be arranged under the prefixes De, De la, Van, Mac, O', etc. [80]

4. Peers to be arranged under their titles, and not under their family names, except in such cases as that of Horace Walpole, where a man is seldom known by his title. Bishops, deans, etc., to be sought under their family names. [87]

5. Sovereigns, saints, and friars to be registered under their Christian names. [91]

6. Latin authors to be registered under their nomens, except in those cases where the agnomen has been popularly adopted. [101]

7. Oriental names to be registered in accordance with the system adopted by a recognized authority on the subject. [95]

8. When an author has changed his name, he is to be registered by the last one adopted. [97]

9. Married women to be registered under their married name, except in those cases where they have only written under their maiden name. [98]

10. When an author has adopted several pseudonyms at various times, all are to be brought together under the

author's true name. When an author
has consistently used one pseudonym,
and is solely known by that name, he
can be registered under it, with a reference from his true name.   [146]

11. Christian names of authors are to
follow their surnames, within parentheses,
and are always to be written in full. [95]

Non-Author Headings.

12. Trials to be entered under the
name of the defendant in a criminal suit,
and of the plaintiff in a civil suit. Trials
relating to vessels to be entered under
the name of the vessel.   [122]

13. Catalogues to be arranged under
the heading of " Catalogues," and subdivided under the sub-headings of the
objects catalogued.   [123]

14. Records of voyages not entirely
written by one author to be brought
under the name of the vessel.   [127]

15. All anonymous books whose authors
are certainly known are to be registered
under those authors' names.   [130]

16. When an author is unknown, and
the initials only are given on the title-

page of a book, or at the end of the preface, dedication, or other preliminary matter, the book is to be considered as anonymous, and treated in accordance with the following rules respecting anonymous works. [145]

17. Anonymous works relating to a person or a place to be registered under the name of that person or place. [131]

18. Anonymous works with a catch-title, such as the title of a novel, to be registered under the first word of that title. [131]

19. Other anonymous works to be registered under the name of the subject which is prominently referred to on the title-page, and in the language of the title-page. An adjective is frequently to be preferred to a substantive as a heading. For instance, when it contains the point of the compound, as *Alimentary* Canal, *English* History, etc. [131]

The Title.

20. The title of a book when not long is to be taken in its entirety. When long curtailment must be undertaken with care,

and dots should be inserted where words
have been omitted. [133]

21. Information respecting the edition
and the editor, and any additional matter,
should be included in the catalogue slip.
[160]

PLACE OF PUBLICATION.

22. The place of publication must
always be given, and if it be not found
on the title-page, it must be added
between brackets whenever known. The
name always to be given as it appears
on the title-page. Sometimes the place
of printing, when different from that of
publication, is added, but this is only
necessary in rare cases. [163]

DATE.

23. Dates are always to be given in a
catalogue in Arabic numerals. It is important that the date should be discovered
when it does not occur on the title-page.
The date may sometimes occur as a
chronogram, which should not be overlooked. [164]

24. Greek dates require special attention.
For a table of these see Chapter IV., p. 167.

Size-Notation.

25. In books published before the use of machine-made papers, the size of books is to be distinguished by the signatures and the fold of the water-mark of the hand-made paper. In modern books demy octavo is to be considered as the standard of an octavo. All above that size to be styled large octavo, and all below small octavo. Quartos and folios to be so designated, except in those cases where they are either specially large or specially small, when they should respectively be described as large quarto or small folio.   [168]

Collation.

26. In the case of rare books a collation should be added to the title slip; but all books, when only in one volume, should have the number of their pages added. [178]

Abstracts of Contents.

27. When the contents of a set of works are very varied, a short abstract of the contents of each volume may be added

with advantage. When the contents are of a similar character, like a collection of plays, it will be more convenient to throw the titles into alphabetical order, and add the number of the volume to each entry. [206]

REFERENCES.

28. All references should be in English, and the subject of a book must be referenced, even if it is not clearly expressed on the title-page. [187]

29. When a book contains something which is not mentioned on the title-page, it must be added either between brackets or in a note, and then a reference can be made to it; but no reference must be made to a title which does not contain the information required. [187]

30. References in an alphabetical catalogue should not be classified. Thus Gold should be under G, and Silver under S, instead of being grouped under Metals. Cross-references may be given from Metals to Gold and Silver. [188]

31. It is not necessary to follow the exact wording of a title in the reference but it will be often more convenient for

16

the cataloguer to make a heading which may include several references.   [187]

32. Before arranging the entries of a catalogue it will be necessary to decide whether all the books are to be included in one alphabet; and if not, what are to be excluded.   [209]

33. Pamphlets or tracts should not be catalogued separately from the other books, except in very special cases. [210]

34. If a library contains many magazines or journals, transactions of societies, or astronomical and other observations, it will be well to keep these distinct from the general catalogue; but if they are few, they can be included in the general alphabet.   [211]

35. Transactions of societies should be arranged under the name of the place where the society holds its meetings, and these names should be arranged in alphabetical order.   [219]

36. When a society has shifted its place of meeting, all its publications should be entered under the name of the existing

place, with references from the names of the previous places of meeting. [223]

37. Journals should be arranged in alphabetical order under the first word of the title not an article. [225]

38. Journals not to be placed under the editors' names. [226]

39. Astronomical and meteorological observations should be kept distinct from transactions of societies, but they may be arranged in the same way under the names of the places where the observatories are situated. [226]

Alphabet.

40. The arrangement to be according to the order of the English alphabet. I and J, U and V, to be treated as separate letters. [198]

41. In German names ä, ö, ü to be treated as if written a, o, u. If it be desired to arrange them as ae, oe, ue, they must be so written. [199]

42. The prefixes Mr., Mc, St., etc., should be arranged as if spelt Mister, Mac, Saint, etc. [200]

43. When the word *Saint* represents

a ceremonial title, as in the case of St. Alban, St. Giles, and St. Augustine, these names are to be arranged under the letters A and G respectively; but the places St. Albans, St. Giles, and St. Augustines should be found under the prefix Saint. [201]

44. Prefixes in proper names, even when printed separately, are to be treated as if they were joined. Thus De Morgan will come before Demosthenes, and De Quincey after Demosthenes. [205]

45. Headings consisting of two or more distinct words are not to be treated as integral portions of one word. [205]

Order of Sub-Entries.

46. The works of an author should be arranged in the following order :—

a. Collected works.

b. Partial collections.

c. Separate works in chronological order, except in the case of plays or novels, which may be in alphabetical order.

d. Translations in the same order as that adopted for the original works. [205]

MANIPULATION.

47. Slips of paper or thick cards should be used for writing the titles upon. A convenient size is that of a page of note paper used lengthways. The shelf-mark can be placed at the top of the right-hand corner. The author's name or heading should be written on a line by itself at the left-hand side, about an inch from the top of the paper.

48. The references may be written upon similar slips, so as to range with the titles.

49. Various directions as to sorting have been given, but the worker will soon find out for himself the most convenient mode. The arrangement should be made in regular sequence. Thus the slips must be sorted into first letters, then into second letters, and so on.

50. When the slips are sorted, it will be necessary to place them in boxes or drawers for safety.

51. If the slips are sent to the printer, they must be numbered ; but when there are a large number, it is not necessary to put the full number on each slip. It

will be sufficient to number up to one hundred, and then begin again, marking down each additional hundred. The alphabetical order of the slips will check the numbering.

52. When a catalogue is printed, lines of repetition must be used if the author's name or other heading is the same in several entries. This line should not be too long, as it is a mistake to vary its length to denote the length of that which is repeated. [201]

53. The usual form for the library copy of a catalogue is folio. If the catalogue is in manuscript, the left-hand page should in all cases be left vacant for additions, and the entries on the right-hand page should not be too closely written, as it is difficult to tell how many additions may be required before the catalogue is worn out. In the case of a printed catalogue, two pages of print can be pasted on one page, and here the right-hand column should be left blank for additions.

APPENDIX.

HE cataloguer will often find it difficult to tell where a book was printed in those cases where the name of the place is given in its Latin form. Although books have been compiled to give this information, they are not always at hand, and a list of the Latin names of some of the most important places where books have been printed will probably be found useful. The same place has often several Latin forms, as will be seen by this list :—

Aberdonia, Aberdeen.
Abredea, Aberdeen.
Abredonia, Aberdeen.
Amstelœdamum, *Amstelodamum*, or *Amstelredamum*, Amsterdam.
Andegavum, Angers.
Andoverpa, Antwerp.
Andreapolis, St. Andrews.
Antverpia, Antwerp.

Ardmacha, Armagh.
Argentina, Argentoratum, Strasburg.
Athenæ Rauracæ, Basel.
Augusta Taurinorum, Turin.
Augusta Trebocorum, Strasburg.
Augusta Trevirorum, Treves.
Augusta Vindelicorum, Augsburg.
Aurelia, Aureliacum, Orleans.
Aurelia Allobrogum, Geneva.

Bamberga, Babenberga, Bamberg.
Barchino, Barcino, or *Barxino,* Barcelona.
Basilea, Basel.
Bathonia, Bath.
Berolinum, Berlin.
Bipontium, Zweibrücken.
Bisuntia, or *Bisuntium,* Besançon.
Bononia, Bologna.
Brixia, Breschia.
Brugæ, Bruges.
Bruxellæ, Bruxelles.
Burdigala, Bordeaux.
Burgi, Burgos.
Buscum Ducis, Bois le Duc, or Hertogenbosch.

Cadomum, Caen.
Cæsar Augusta, Saragossa.
Cæsarodunum Turonum, Tours.
Cameracum, Cambray.
Cantabrigia, Cambridge.

Casurgis, Prague.
Cluniacum, Cluni.
Coburgum, Coburg,
Codania, Copenhagen.
Colonia Agrippina, *C. Claudia*, *C. Ubiorum*
or *Colonia* simply, Cologne.
Colonia Allobrogum, Geneva.
Colonia Julia Romana, Seville.
Colonia Munatiana, Basel.
Complutum, Alcala de Henares, famous as
the place of printing of the Polyglott
Bible of Cardinal Ximenes, called the
" Complutensian Bible."
Confluentes, Coblentz.
Cracovia, Cracow.
Curia Rhetorum, Coire.

Dantiscum, Dantzig.
Daventria, Deventer, in Holland.
Derbia, Derby.
Dordracum, Dordrecht, or Dort.
Dresda, Dresden.
Duacum, Douay.
Dublinum, Dublin.
Durocorturum, Rheims.

Eboracum, York.
Edinburgum, Edinburgh.
Erfordia, *Erphordia*, or *Erfurtum*, Erfurt.
Etona, Eton.
Exonia, Exeter.

Florentia, Florence.
Forum Livii, Forli.
Francofurtum ad Mœnum, Francofortium, Francphordia, Frankfort-on-the-Maine.
Francofurtum ad Oderam, or *Francophordia cis Oderam,* or *Francofurtum Marchionum,* Frankfort-on-the-Oder.
Freiberga Hermundurorum, Freiberg, Saxony.
Friburgum Brisgoviæ, Freiburg im Breisgau.
Friburgum Helvetiorum, Fribourg, Switzerland.

Ganabum, Orleans.
Gandavum, Gand, or Ghent.
Gedanum, Dantzig.
Genua, Genoa.
Gippesvicum, Ipswich.
Glascua, Glasgow.
Granata, Granada.
Gratianopolis, Grenoble.
Gravionarium, Bamberg.

Hafnia, Copenhagen.
Haga Comitum, The Hague.
Hala Saxonum, Hala Hermundurorum, Hala Soraborum, or *Hala Magdeburgica,* Halle, in Saxony.
Hamburgum, or *Hammona,* Hamburg.
Harlemum, Haarlem.
Heidelberga, Heidelberg.

Helenopolis, Frankfort-on-the-Maine.
Herbipolis, Würzburg.
Hispalis, Seville.
Holmia, Stockholm.

Insulæ, Lisle.

Juliomagum, Angers.

Koburgum, Coburg.

Leida, Leyden.
Leodicum Eburonum, Liege.
Leodium, Liege.
Lipsia, Leipzig.
Londinum, Londinium, London.
Lovanium, Louvain.
Lugdunum, Lyons.
Lugdunum Batavorum, Leyden.
Lutetia Parisiorum, Paris.

Madritum, or *Matritum,* Madrid.
Mediolanum, Milan.
Moguntia, Mentz, or Mayence.
Monachium, Munich.
Mons Regius, Königsberg.
Moscua, Moscow.
Mutina, Modena.

Neapolis, Naples.

Neocomum, Neuchatel.
Norimberga, Nuremberg.

Œnipons, Innsbruck.
Olyssipo, Lisbon.
Oxonia, or *Oxonium,* Oxford.

Panormum, Palermo.
Papia, Pavia.
Parisii, Paris.
Patavium, Padua.
Pons Œni, Innsbruck.
Portus Lusitaniæ, Oporto.
Praga, Prague.

Regiomontum, Königsberg.
Remi, or *Rhemi,* Rheims.
Rhedones, Rennes.
Rhodopolis, Rostock.
Roma, Rome.
Rostochium, Rostock.
Rothomagum, Rouen.

S. Albani, St. Albans.
Sanctandrois, St. Andrews.
Sylva Ducis, or *Sylva Ducalis,* Bois le Duc,
    or Hertogenbosch.

Tarvisium, Treviso.
Taurinum, Turin.

Thermæ Antoninæ, Baden-Baden.
Ticinum, Pavia.
Tigurum, Zürich.
Toletum, Toledo.
Trajectum ad Mosam, or *Trajectum superius*,
  Maestricht.
Trajectum ad Rhenum, or *Trajectum inferius*,
  Utrecht.
Trajectum ad Viadrum, Frankfort-on-thè-
  Oder.
Trecæ, or *Tricasses*, Troyes.
Tridentum, Trent.
Treviri, Treves.
Tubinga, Tubingen.
Turones, Tours.

Ubii, Cologne.
Ultrajectum, Utrecht.
Ulyssipo, Lisbon.
Urbs vetus, Orvieto.

Vallisoletum, Valladolid.
Venetiæ, Venice.
Vesontio, Besancon.
Vicentia, Vicenza.
Vienna Austriæ, Vienna.
Vienna in Delphinatu, Vienne, France.
Vigornia, Worcester.
Vindobona, Vienna.
Vratislavia, Breslau.

Westmonasterium, Westminster.
Wirceburgum, Wurzburg.

These names have mostly been taken from Dr. Cotton's valuable lists :—

A Typographical Gazetteer, attempted by the Rev. Henry Cotton, D.C.L. The Second Edition. Oxford, 1831. 8vo.

At page 332 is an index of disguised, falsified, or fictitious places.

At page 336, a list of the names of certain academies, etc., which sometimes are found on the titles of books (particularly on academical dissertations), without further specification of the place to which they belong.

A Typographical Gazetteer, attempted by the Rev. Henry Cotton, D.C.L. Second Series. Oxford, 1866. 8vo.

At page 335 is a revised list of fictitious places.

INDEX.

17

For EU product safety concerns, contact us at Calle de José Abascal, 56–1°,
28003 Madrid, Spain or eugpsr@cambridge.org.

www.ingramcontent.com/pod-product-compliance
Ingram Content Group UK Ltd.
Pitfield, Milton Keynes, MK11 3LW, UK
UKHW010346140625
459647UK00010B/859